THE HOUSE YOUR STARS BUILT

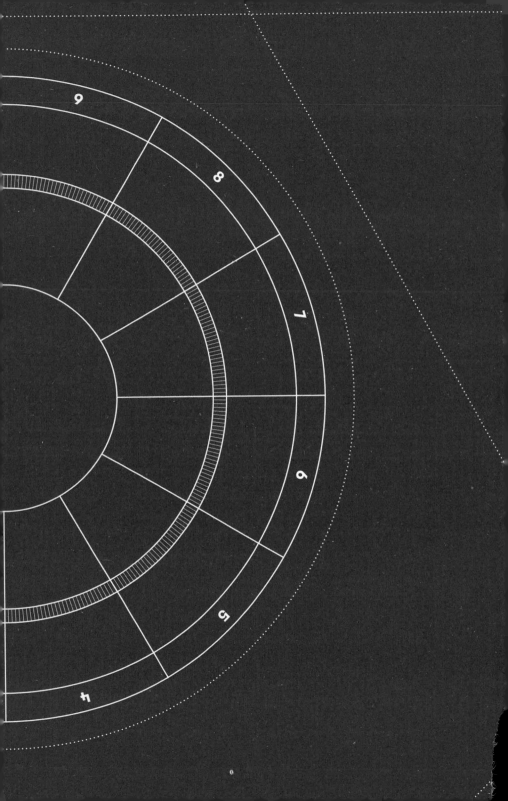

THE HOUSE

YOUR STARS

BUILT

✦

A GUIDE TO THE TWELVE
ASTROLOGICAL HOUSES & YOUR
PLACE IN THE UNIVERSE

✦

Rachel Stuart-Haas

TILLER PRESS

NEW YORK   LONDON   TORONTO   SYDNEY   NEW DELHI

An Imprint of Simon & Schuster, Inc.
1230 Avenue of the Americas
New York, NY 10020

Text copyright © 2021 by Simon & Schuster, Inc.

Illustrations copyright © 2021 by Rachel Stuart-Haas

First Tiller Press hardcover edition March 2021

TILLER PRESS and colophon are trademarks of Simon & Schuster, Inc.

For information about special discounts for bulk purchases,
please contact Simon & Schuster Special Sales at 1-866-506-1949
or business@simonandschuster.com.

The Simon & Schuster Speakers Bureau can bring authors to your
live event. For more information or to book an event, contact the
Simon & Schuster Speakers Bureau at 1-866-248-3049 or visit our
website at www.simonspeakers.com.

Interior design by Matthew Ryan
Halfmoon symbol, star symbol, and degree lines by Shutterstock

Manufactured in the United States of America

3   5   7   9   10   8   6   4   2

Library of Congress Cataloging-in-Publication Data
Names: Stuart-Haas, Rachel, author.
Title: The house your stars built : a guide to the twelve astrological
houses and your place in the universe / Rachel Stuart-Haas.
Description: New York : Tiller Press, [2021]
Identifiers: LCCN 2020044790 (print) | LCCN 2020044791 (ebook) |
ISBN 9781982164867 (hardcover) | ISBN 9781982164874 (ebook)
Subjects: LCSH: Birth charts. | Zodiac. | Astrology.
Classification: LCC BF1719 .S77 2021 (print) | LCC BF1719 (ebook) |
DDC 133.5--dc23

ISBN 978-1-9821-6486-7
ISBN 978-1-9821-6487-4 (ebook)

CONTENTS

INTRODUCTION

Hello!
Buckle up (keep your hands, arms, feet, and legs inside the ride at all times) because we're off on a journey into the fascinating—and let's face it—rather intimidating field of astrology. But never fear, I'll be here as a guide to make this trip way less mysterious, and hopefully a lot of fun. By the time you've finished reading, not only will you have acquired the skills to read your own chart (and have a great party trick up your sleeve to impress your friends and family), but you'll have learned a heck of a lot about yourself—from how you love to what you long for, to career fulfillment to the most nurturing forms of self-care. Our stars invite us to pause, turn inward, and see what paths the universe is nudging us to follow.

I don't need to tell you that these are stressful times. We compare ourselves to high standards set by perfectly curated Instagram feeds and glossy magazine pages. Workplaces are rarely secure and turnover is commonplace. Articles about climate change, social inequality, political bad behavior, disease, and natural disaster dominate the headlines and keep us from falling asleep at night. Technology is evolving at a dizzying pace. While we are more globally connected than at any other point in human history, we often feel lonely. It can often seem impossible to build meaningful, deep connections in a "right swipe" society.

Negative stress affects our lives almost daily. It can impact our physical and mental health in so many ways and has become so prevalent, that we tend to just accept it as a normal everyday part of life. We all have ways to get through the day, to keep our heads and hopes high. Besides getting more sleep, taking some deep breaths, and eating a few pieces of chocolate, I've got another tool to keep in your self-care toolkit, a way to find solace and a guide to living your best life: the Stars.

Yep, good old-fashioned astrology.

To practice astrology is to have a *huge* advantage when it comes to facing fears or periods of uncertainty, creating goals, and shaping your future. Forewarned is forearmed, and trust me on this, gaining insight on how the universe affects you can be a rewarding emotional process. Studying astrology brings greater self-knowledge and affirms not only who you are, but who you are evolving into. Most people find reading their charts not just insightful but also deeply therapeutic.

Astrology can point you toward the best time to go for that raise, to take a chance on love, or to simply make time for yourself. You always have free will, of course, but aligning yourself with the energy of the cosmos will give you a leg up on life decisions big or small. Perhaps even more importantly and profoundly, it will help you get to know yourself better. You spend every one of your trips around the sun with yourself. Self-reflection. Self-acceptance. Self-improvement. These are valuable gifts. The gifts of the stars.

So, what exactly is astrology? Quite simply, astrology is the study of planets, stars, and seasons and their impact on humans here on earth. Learning to interpret this information is a lot like learning another language, and it can feel overwhelming at first. But as you learn to decode the astral codes, a door opens up, granting you a backstage pass to the profound influence of the universe on our earthly lives. Instead of learning how to conjugate verbs or say "Where is the bathroom," this ancient language will help you take part in the primordial conversation between the stars, moon, and planets of our universe. Our goal in practicing astrology is to become fluent in the way celestial bodies interact with one another, so that we can interpret how these synergies shape major events in history and our personal journeys.

As far as we can tell, humans have always searched for meaning in the night sky. As evidenced by early cave drawings, even ancient civilizations recognized cycles in the stars and planets and used those patterns to help with quotidian tasks like farming and navigation, as well as guides for spiritual expression. But the roots of modern astrology can be found in ancient Babylonia. Those clever Babylonians noodled out that the constellations appear to move and that these movements worked well as a celestial time gauge if divided into distinguishable and equal segments. Even better, they gave each segment a memorable name. Can we say early branding?

Then the Greeks, who were always a little extra, took the foundation provided by the Babylonians and built on it. One of their contributions was providing us with the term for the ring of constellations first identified by the Babylonians which they labeled *zodiakos kyklos* or literally animal circle.

ZODIAC: Think of the zodiac as a belt around the heavens. It extends a little bit north and south of the path the sun appears to take around the earth over the course of the year. The stars (and constellations) contained within this belt are divided into twelve segments and compose the twelve signs.

While the Greeks were instrumental in helping define the zodiac, over in Egypt, a mathematician named Ptolemy published a book called *Tetrabiblos* which basically took all the cool things people were learning about the stars and their impact on human life (including planets, zodiac signs, houses, and aspects) and put it on paper . . . or shall we say papyrus? The Romans, never ones to resist putting their own stamps on things, gave the names to the zodiac houses (Capricorn, Taurus, Cancer, and so on) we still use today.

After the fall of the Roman Empire, astrology fell out of favor in the West but took off in the great Islamic empires and East Asia where it is still practiced today. In the Middle Ages, astrology again became common in Western civilization. From professors to popes, the greatest minds in Europe applied themselves to the study of the planets. Astrology became a point of contemplation for great thinkers like Carl Jung and others in the nineteenth and twentieth centuries and ubiquitous in newspaper columns. Who didn't consult (or watch their parents consult) their horoscope in the local paper before heading off to work or school in the 1980s and 1990s? And these days, astrology apps are among the most popular in the app store. As far as I'm concerned this is absolutely fabulous, and the fact you're here reading these words is to join the ranks of many wise and/or famous folks who've looked to the stars to help them accomplish their goals.

ASTROLOGY ISN'T JUST FOR MILLENNIALS and New Agey folks! Many celebrities and important historical figures have turned to the stars over the years. Let's take a quick look at a few notable people who have used astrology to inform their strategic decision making and life choices. Here are five examples that might surprise you:

J. P. MORGAN (BANKING TYCOON): Mr. Morgan once famously said that millionaires don't need astrologers, but billionaires do. He thought that there was much more to the market than lucky timing, and often used astrologers to help guide him at critical junctures in his businesses and investments.

NANCY REAGAN (FIRST LADY): After the attempted assassination of President Reagan in 1981, Nancy sought out the services of a notable astrologer whom she consulted in secret. It's rumored that many of Reagan's political decisions were "timed" astrologically despite his denials.

BEN FRANKLIN (FOUNDING FATHER): In 1776, Benjamin Franklin deliberately changed the date members of the Continental Congress signed America's Declaration of Independence. It was originally supposed to occur on July 2, but he pushed to change the date to the 4th to take advantage of the friendlier astrological alignments on that day. So thank the stars next year while you chomp your hot dog while watching the fireworks!

PRINCESS DIANA (PRINCESS OF WALES): Princess Diana openly consulted psychics and astrologers throughout her adult life. According to her personal astrologer, the practice gave her control in a high-profile life that often felt anything but.

CHARLES DE GAULLE (FRENCH GENERAL/ PRESIDENT): After World War II, de Gaulle enlisted the assistance of a major in the French army who was skilled in astrological charts. He consulted the man regularly until losing power after a series of political decisions the astrologer had strongly cautioned against.

Human beings need to feel like we are part of something larger than ourselves, to be connected to the great and mighty universe. Many of us crave a way to make sense out of our lives and to see ourselves as part of a larger plan. Pythagoras, that mathematician whose pesky theorem has tortured many a student, wisely said, "The stars in heaven sing a music if only we had ears to hear." The universe has lessons for us all if only we can open our hearts and be receptive to learning about ourselves.

So, with stars in our eyes and determination in our hearts, let us return to the present day and discover how we can use this rich historical practice in our daily lives.

Part **1**

MEET

the

ASTROLOGY

WHEEL

ASTROLOGY
REFRESHER

1

Perhaps you have glanced at your horoscope on a bleary-eyed Sunday morning after a few too many cocktails. Maybe you not only know your Sun sign, but you're already familiar with your Moon and Rising signs as well. Or perhaps you are picking up this book as a newcomer to this strange and wonderful new world and need a quick primer on the basics. If the former is you, feel free to skip ahead to the next section. But if you're a little nervous and want to brush up before going further, linger a bit and I'll give you the lowdown.

Okay, Rachel, let's start at the beginning . . . All I know about astrology is that cheesy pickup line "Hey, baby, what's your sign?". So, remind me what exactly the signs are again?

Your "sign"—more accurately called your Sun sign—is determined based on where the Sun was stationed in the Astrology Wheel when you were born. Don't worry! We'll come back to that Astrology Wheel in a minute. What you need to know now is that there are twelve possibilities:

ARIES (Those born March 21–April 19)

TAURUS (April 20–May 20)

GEMINI (May 21–June 20)

CANCER (June 21–July 22)

LEO (July 23–August 22)

VIRGO (August 23–September 22)

LIBRA (September 23–October 22)

SCORPIO (October 23–November 21)

SAGITTARIUS (November 22–December 21)

CAPRICORN (December 22–January 19)

AQUARIUS (January 20–February 18)

PISCES (February 19–March 20)

Okay, so now you know your sign. But didn't you say they stand for animals or something? And if they are part of a classic cheesy pickup line, I'm guessing that means it's important in some way?
Yes and yes! Each zodiac has a set of personality traits, tendencies, and qualities attributed to it, so your Sun sign is important because it helps reveal your joys, hopes, flaws, and fears. Later, when we combine the Sun sign with the other planets in your chart, it's going to help create the distinctive profile that serves as your astrological fingerprint. After all, there are currently 7.5 billion people living on this blue and green planet in a relatively minor outer spiral of the Milky Way galaxy, and only twelve zodiac signs. So the Sun sign gives some insight, but you'll need to go deeper to get to the good stuff. But as a rule, here's some high-level information just to get you grounded:

ARIES (Symbol: The Ram): As the zodiac's first sign, you've got a little bit of that whole "Imma Numba Onnnnnnnnne" thing going on. When everyone's ready to go home for the night, you're just getting started. Careful, your energy might exhaust others, or be seen as too aggressive, but that's the life of a trailblazer. Just like your namesake, you're going to ram your way toward your goals.

> **Most likely to do an internet search on:**
> "Best Local Hiking Trails" or "Krav Maga Studios."

TAURUS (Symbol: The Bull): Just like your animal namesake, you have two speeds: either grazing peacefully in the pasture, or stampeding head down through the streets of Pamplona. Midday naps? Yes, please! But when the going gets hard, you'll pull an all-nighter. Sure you're stubborn, but that strong work ethic is how you get things done. Just be sure not to get stuck in routines that don't serve you well and it doesn't hurt to let go of a grudge sometimes (no, really, come on, that happened *fifteen years* ago!). At the end of the day, everyone is rooting for you to charge forward and live your best life.

> **Most likely to do an internet search on:**
> "How to Work Smarter, Not Harder."

GEMINI (Symbol: The Twins): Who says having a split personality is bad? Certainly not you, Gemini! It just means you're extra. You're bound to attract attention and everywhere you go you're bound to run into acquaintances. If anyone has to take a cross-country road trip, you're the one they want in the passenger seat. Not only will you have the latest phone, the perfectly curated playlist, all the coolest podcasts, you'll also be able to talk a mile a minute all the way through flyover country. The problem is you can flip the switch, get depressed, overwhelmed, and sometimes a little two-faced. Being in your orbit can be a roller-coaster ride of ups and downs, but it's sure never boring.

> **Most likely to do an internet search on:**
> "Best New Political Podcasts to Check Out."

CANCER (Symbol: The Crab): With those power claws, you sensitive crabs hold on tight to the things that matter, be it a loved one, a home, or the sense of security. Change might send you scuttling for safety, but if you are given the space and opportunity to nurture your creative, compassionate, and helpful side, you're going to thrive no matter the size of the breaking waves.

> **Most likely to do an internet search on:**
> "Interior Decorating Ideas."

LEO (Symbol: The Lion): All attention is good attention, am I right, Leo? Just kidding, we all love you even if you're not exactly the humble type. Your dramatic ways always make a statement, but your natural-born leadership skills are always on point. If there's a competition afoot, other folks better watch out, as you're quick to pounce. At times egotistical or self-centered, if you can remember those lessons from kindergarten and take turns, play nice, and share, you're going to do just fine.

> **Most likely to do an internet search on:**
> "Best Instagram Filter."

VIRGO (Symbol: The Virgin): You're the observant one of the bunch, quick to size up a room and ready to spring into action to pitch in where it's needed most. Micromanaging is your downfall. Take a chill pill, down a kale smoothie, and remember sometimes it's A-OK to ask for help when it's needed. Other people may laugh at how you feel compelled to clutter bust during moments of stress, but let them. You know you find your inner Zen in a perfectly curated bookshelf or by arranging your teas in alphabetical order.

> **Most likely to do an internet search on:**
> "How to Organize My Pantry."

LIBRA (Symbol: The Scales): Hey smooth talker, you know how to love the finer things in life and love to indulge in the kitchen. Gallery opening? Farm-to-table menus? Silk sheets? Linen hand towels? Jo Malone candles? That's your jam. Balance is your game and anything unfair throws you off-kilter . . . you simply can't tolerate it. Good thing you pack charm in spades and if you don't take a "my way or the highway" approach, then you'll be able to charm your way into the result of your choice.

> **Most likely to do an internet search on:**
> "Best YouTube Hacks."

SCORPIO (Symbol: The Scorpion): You sweet, sensitive soul (and secret control freak), you are just always in your feelings, huh? You are the seductive, intense one, who draws others in with their magnetic energy. Try not to lash out and use that painful sting when you get hurt. It takes a lot for you to trust enough to get vulnerable, and when you do, you're sticking with your people through all the seasons. Voted most likely to love *Fifty Shades of Grey*, or at least be intrigued by the bondage aspects.

> **Most likely to do an internet search on:**
> "Recommended Erotic Fiction."

SAGITTARIUS (Symbol: The Archer): Sag, my dear, you love to shoot for the stars, don't ya? You thrive on starting a new project or an endeavor. The new and shiny gets you going. But remember not to get overconfident or flaky. We're going to see you booking long-haul flights to see the world, flirting at the bar, and singing your heart out in karaoke. Everyone loves your inappropriate jokes, but try not to be too tactless.

> **Most likely to do an internet search on:**
> "Best Travel Deals."

CAPRICORN (Symbol: The Goat): You Capricorns are an ambitious lot, eager to scale impossible mountains, but doing so one cautious hoof step at a time. You work harder than anyone and keep your head down to get to the good stuff you know is right around the corner. Word to the wise: not every effort needs to be a struggle. Sometimes it's okay to flick your tail, toss your horns, and scamper around for the fun of it. And when you get to the top of those mountains, for Pete's sake, take a second to enjoy it, will ya?

> **Most likely to do an internet search on:**
> "Improving My LinkedIn Profile."

AQUARIUS (Symbol: The Water Bearer): You do you, Aquarius! You're a true original who marches to your own beat. Getting involved in social justice issues, or science and tech are often fulfilling career pathways, and personal freedom is important to you. While you might be a fun and free-spirited friend, behind the scenes close lovers and family might sneak a peek at a more neurotic and anxious side. To keep it groovy you need to strike a balance between the quirk and your Type A tendencies.

> **Most likely to do an internet search on:**
> "Volunteer Opportunities in My Community."

PISCES (Symbol: The Fish): Ah, Pisces, you slippery little dreamer, you. You're always trying to dart away and escape reality. Many people born under this sign are intensely imaginative lovers of film, fine wine, and music. Careful, though, there can be a tendency for these romantic and idealistic folks to have a bit of a "tortured soul" quality that can be self-destructive. Keep at least one fin firm in the real world, and recharge yourself with meditation and creative pursuits.

> **Most likely to do an internet search on:**
> "Must-See Films by Decade."

When I'm reading my chart, am I supposed to look at my Sun? Moon? asteroids? planets? black holes? or what?

In short, yes. But since we're just learning, we're going to be focusing on the Sun, Moon, and planets during this book.

> **PLUTO:** Back in 2006, astronomers stripped Pluto of its official planet status. It's orbiting way out there on the edge of our solar system, but that doesn't mean it doesn't affect us. Therefore, for the purposes of astrological influence, it's still considered a planet.

Depending on when you were born, these planets will fall into one of the twelve houses.

i'm still confused. What is the difference between houses and signs?

Don't worry, this part can be a little tricky for some folks. We're going to get more into houses in the next chapter.

Is a natal chart like a horoscope?

A natal chart is also called a birth chart. It's an astrological snapshot of the planets, Sun, Moon, and other celestial bodies at your moment of birth. Natal astrology believes that the influence of the cosmos at your moment of birth sets the pattern for the lifetime. Less common terms for it are "geniture" and "nativity," which have mostly fallen into disuse. Your horoscope is a current view of your natal chart for the day, week, or month. It's a snapshot of your current place in the universe. The actual word "horoscope" is derived from the Latin combination of two words in which "horo" means hour and "scope" means view, so it is a "view of the hour."

Can astrology be used in other ways besides the personal horoscope?

Yes! Astrology can be used to predict times of social change, political unrest, periods of human history. It can also be used to determine auspicious times to get married and experience a life cycle event. You can even use astrology to find out an answer to a specific question that may be plaguing you. In this book, we're going to be focused on natal astrology or gaining understanding about a person based on where the stars were located when they were born.

ARE THERE OTHER KINDS OF ASTROLOGY BESIDES NATAL?

MUNDANE (term is coined from Latin word "mundus"): Branch of astrology concerned primarily with geographical regions.

ELECTIONAL (aka event astrology): Electional astrology is used to decide when the most appropriate time is for an event based on the astrological auspiciousness of that time.

HORARY: A way to hack life's big questions without getting into a complex birth chart. Horary astrologers might look for the influence of just one or two planets. It's basically a form of divination: seeking knowledge from the future.

I hear people talk about the term cusp? What is that all about?

It refers to the border between either the signs of the zodiac or the twelve houses on your natal chart.

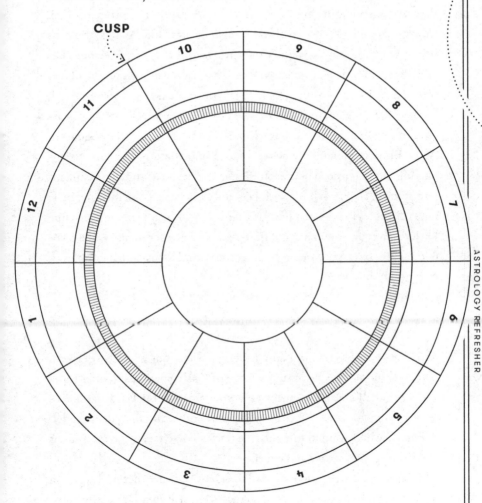

The word "cusp" is used in astrology. The most common way is to use it as describing the beginning of a specific house. This is the basis for determining the planetary rulers of the houses in your chart (lots more of this in a bit). When the cusp (beginning) of a certain house falls in a certain sign of the zodiac, the planet that rules that sign of the zodiac is said to become the ruler of the house. There is no such thing as a sign cusp. A planet is either in one sign or another.

What is the Age of Aquarius anyway? Is that a real thing?

Popularized as a song in the musical *Hair*, the Age of Aquarius is indeed real, and we're all living within it. Okay, so every 2,150 years or so, the sun's position during the Northern Hemisphere's spring equinox (March 20) moves to a new zodiac constellation. The Age of Aquarius began when the sun moved on the spring equinox from the constellation Pisces into the constellation Aquarius. Every person on the planet was affected by this shift (debate is rife on the exact year it occurred, but it's often thought to be 2011). The Piscean Age was a time of hierarchy, and knowing where you were on the pecking order. The Aquarian Age will be dominated by networks and information. We can see this playing out in tensions between religion and science, and increasing interest in working to achieve social equality and stamp out inequity in its many forms. My personal hope is that this will be a transcendent time for humanity as we set aside differences over gender identity, the color of our skin, or the size of our bank account and focus on what unites us more than divides us.

....

Astrology can be used in many different ways, but when I work with people I find one of the most precious gifts astrology has to offer is the deeper understanding of ourselves—what fills our bucket, what makes us tick, what allows us to live more authentically. And that, dear reader, is exactly why I wanted to write this book. To give you the tools to interpret your very own natal chart.

Perhaps later you will choose to take things further and work on understanding the planets' ever-changing transit to a DIY daily horoscope, but for now let's start with the natal chart and how it can help you figure out who you are as a person.

In the past, those who wished to understand their own natal chart had to consult a professional astrologer. Big fat books of star locations needed to be consulted. Careful angles had to be drawn. It was not a walk in the park, people! Luckily, we're in the Age of Aquarius (and the digital age) and that makes things oh so much easier.

Yes, thanks to the internet, generating your own personal natal chart these days only takes a few minutes. Do a quick search of "create a natal chart" and select whatever you like best. I prefer astro.com but there are lots of great options. To create your natal chart, you'll need your birthdate, place of birth, and the exact time you entered the world.

DETERMINING YOUR BIRTH TIME CAN BE TRICKY as not everyone knows the exact moment one was born. Maybe you have your birth certificate handy or one of your parents has a really good memory. But for those who can't find it, not to worry, there are still many ways to read your chart! First, you can contact the local Birth Registry Office at your birth town. If that doesn't work, there are many great astrologers out there that can rectify your chart just by looking at major past events in your life and lining them up to match what time you were most likely born. And if all of this seems too much, you can get relatively close by looking up when the sun rose on the day of your birth. Some of the information won't be 100 percent exact, but you can still glean loads of useful information.

So go ahead, get on the internet and print out your chart or just pull it up on your phone, whatever is easiest. Don't worry, I'll be waiting right here.

Do you have your natal chart in hand? Cool! This is an important first step. But our work is just beginning. Deciphering what it says is a whole other ball of wax. All those symbols and lines . . . It sure can look confusing, right? Not to worry, each chapter in this book is going to take you on a journey through your chart as we travel together around the Sun and the houses of the zodiac. Along the way, we're going to unpack the language of astrology and become more comfortable with the basic structure of the Astrology Wheel.

All of these planets and signs are depicted by strange and alien-looking glyphs, so here's a handy chart to make it way less confusing.

AQUARIUS

ARIES

CANCER

GEMINI

JUNO

JUPITER

MERCURY

MOON

NEPTUNE

SAGITTARIUS

SATURN

SCORPIO

VENUS

VESTA

VIRGO

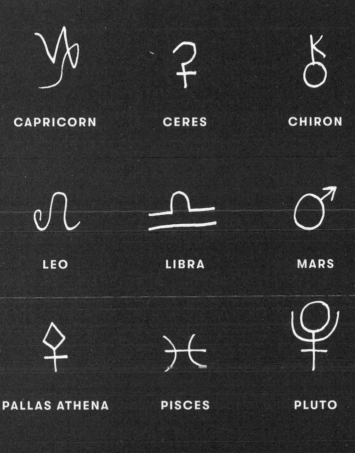

CAPRICORN	CERES	CHIRON
LEO	LIBRA	MARS
PALLAS ATHENA	PISCES	PLUTO
SUN	TAURUS	URANUS

TIP: Feel free to stick a bookmark into this page because unless you have a photographic memory you'll be flipping back here a lot to refer to the glyphs.

PLANETS &
THEIR MEANINGS

Each planet symbolizes a universal component of our lived experiences. They rule over different parts of our essential nature and, depending on where they appear in your chart, they bring different gifts and challenges.

SUN, MOON, PLUTO—PLANETS?

In astrology, "planets" are used to describe those luminary bodies that affect us here on Planet Earth. So that includes the Sun, Moon, and even poor Pluto who got kicked out of the official planet club.

SUN
Represents: Consciousness, Ego, Strength, Resilience

MOON
Represents: Unconsciousness, Feelings, Habits

MERCURY
Represents: Communication, Intellect, Reason, Acumen, Intelligence

VENUS
Represents: Attraction, Love, Harmony, Relationships, Tranquility, Art, Beauty

MARS
Represents: Sex, Desire, Courage, Passion

JUPITER
Represents: Abundance, Growth, Optimism, Understanding

SATURN
Represents: Rigidity, Obligation, Ambition

NEPTUNE
Represents: Dreams, Mysticism, Imagination, Fantasy

URANUS
Represents: Transformation, Fickle, Nonconformity, Eccentricity

PLUTO
Represents: Death, Rebirth, Evolution

Newly armed with a basic understanding of astrology and a basic road map, we're ready to set out on a wonderful journey of self-discovery. So what are we waiting for? Let's dive in and see what the universe has in store!

THE ASTROLOGY WHEEL

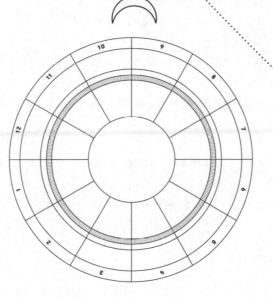

I know you have your natal chart safely in hand but let's take a step back and consider the Astrology Wheel, an awe-inspiring and overwhelming sight. It's our guide to unlock the mysteries contained within ourselves. But exactly what are we even looking at here anyway? Pie slices from outer space? No? A wacky color wheel from *Alice in Wonderland*? Not at all. To begin to unpack what you are seeing in the Astrology Wheel, focus on three basic factors: planets, signs, and houses.

The Astrology Wheel is divided into twelve man-made houses. These "pizza wedge" shapes each represent 30 degrees of a 360-degree whole. Houses are important because they ground the significance of cosmic events back down here on earth. Think of the houses as the walls of "The House Your Stars Built." They provide the structure. Each of these houses represents a different part of your life, ranging from your ego, to your health, to how you attract money and relationships, and everything in between.

The astrological chart provides the structure on which we each overlay our individual natal charts. Remember that the natal chart represents where the planets were in their journey around the Sun at the moment of your birth. So, when you are looking at your natal chart, you are using the Astrology Wheel to see a snapshot of the earth's sky at the exact moment you were born.

Take a look at yours.

This is *your* personal blueprint. So unless you were born in the same location, on the same day, at the same moment as someone else, your wheel will look different from anyone else's. Each chart is unique and special just like each of us on earth is unique and special.

Once you know how to interpret what your astrological natal chart has to say, you can take a deep dive into your unique traits and tendencies, your personality and your strengths, and your weaknesses. Excited? Me too, and we're just about to get to that!

But first . . . a little more background.

THE FOUR MAIN ANGLES
IN A CHART

Within the circle of the horoscope there are four all-important points that define a birth chart in a most special way. They are the cusp (beginning) of the First, Fourth, Seventh, and Tenth houses. These angles are the four Cardinal Points of an astrological chart: the Ascendant, the Midheaven, the Descendant, and the Imum Coeli.

WHY ARE THEY CALLED "CARDINAL POINTS"?

Cardinal directions are the four main points on a compass (North, South, East, West) and those correspond to where these angles are located on your natal chart.

The angles represent where you meet and interact with the outside world. You can think of the angles on the natal chart as a cross of matter, because you can draw a horizontal line connecting the First and Seventh houses, and then a vertical line connecting the Fourth and Tenth houses.

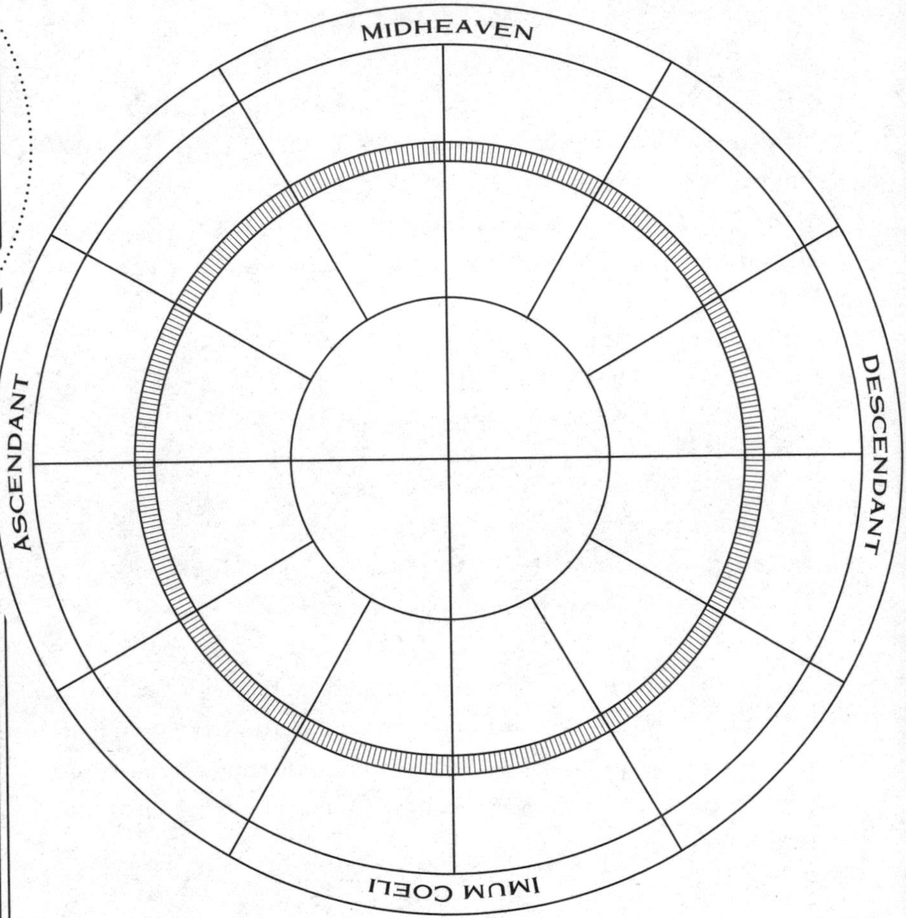

MIDHEAVEN

ASCENDANT

DESCENDANT

IMUM COELI

So, what do the angles in a birth chart mean for you? Let's begin with the Ascendant and then move counterclockwise around the wheel. The Ascendant is also known as the Rising Sign. The Rising Sign is the version of yourself that you project to the world, but it's not always the real *you*. Your Rising is often used in conjunction with your Sun and Moon signs to do a 30,000-foot view of how the stars make you unique as a human during this precious lifetime you've been given.

The Ascendant (Rising Sign) is the zodiac sign that was on the eastern horizon at your moment of birth. A good way to remember Ascendant is that it relates to the part of the sky where the Sun rises, and affects how your appearance and outward presence "dawns" on people. You'll learn more about your personal Ascendant when we examine the zodiac sign that's on the cusp of your first house, but a helpful way to remember it is "First House, first impressions." This part of the chart is your own personal book cover, and you know how people love to judge a book by its cover.

As we move near the Fourth House we come across the next of the four major angles, the IC or Imum Coeli. Imum Coeli is Latin for "Bottom of the Sky"—no surprise there because the IC reveals your roots and foundation. This important angle shows how you were nurtured as a child and how you feel nurtured in life. This is a place where you explore those deep—and sometimes dark—parts of yourself that you probably don't often reveal to others. It's who you are when you're alone, vegged out in your comfort zone, far away from the glare of the public eye. When we take a deep dive into the Fourth House, you're going to want to pay careful attention to who your ruler is there.

The next angle we come across is the DC or Descendant. This point is located directly across the wheel from your Ascendant and on the cusp of your Seventh House. It's where you're going to want to look for information on the sorts of people you attract and what sort of partner suits you best.

And lastly, we come to the very top of the wheel to the Midheaven, or Medium Coeli. This shows your career or how you want to be known in the world. It's your public reputation. It's on the cusp of your Tenth House, directly across the wheel from your Immum Coeli. If the Fourth House is the most private and out of view, the Tenth is where you can get a sense of what comforts you and creates a sense of home.

Think of the Cardinal Points as a quick Cliff's Notes section of a chart. And don't worry, we're going to soon see the influence of the zodiac on each of your houses, and then after that, how the planets are making their impact.

THE TWELVE HOUSES
AT A GLANCE

FIRST HOUSE: Self, Appearance, Persona, Health

SECOND HOUSE: Values, Possessions, Finances, Self-Worth

THIRD HOUSE: Communication, Mentality, Siblings, Short Trips

FOURTH HOUSE: Home and Family, Real Estate, Parents (usually the father), Old Age

FIFTH HOUSE: Pleasure, Children, Romance, Gambling

SIXTH HOUSE: Healthy, Organization and Routine, Small Pets

SEVENTH HOUSE: Relationships, Who You Attract, Marriage

EIGHTH HOUSE: Transformation, Sex, Taxes, Taboo, Partners, Money, Shared Energy, Death and Rebirth

NINTH HOUSE: Philosophy, Religion, Long-Distance Travel, How Others Talk to You, Higher Education

TENTH HOUSE: Status, Career, Parents (usually the mother)

ELEVENTH HOUSE: Friendship, Community, Hopes and Wishes

TWELFTH HOUSE: Spirituality, Unconscious, Psychic Gifts and All Things Hidden

The Astrology Wheel sets the stage for the planets and how they interact with one another. It's the crucial backdrop that connects the constellations with asteroids, comets, and planets and provides the visualization we need to see how they all interact. The chart as a whole is important, but if you want a quick snapshot remember to take a look at the Sun, Moon, and Ascendant (or better yet, the Sun, Moon, and those four Cardinal Points from up above). This will give you lightning-fast clues as to how you operate. True, you're not going to see the minute details, but what you will discover is oh so revealing! Look at these three things FIRST:

THE SUN SIGN in a chart reveals who you are in this lifetime and what you are here to do—by sign and by house. If you don't honor your Sun sign, you'll never feel fulfilled. It's crucial to focus on that Sun!

THE MOON SIGN shows how you nurture yourself, and in turn how you were nurtured as a child. It'll show what you *need*, how you make yourself comfy, and how you can nourish yourself when you're down in the dumps.

THE ASCENDANT/RISING SIGN shows the direction you are going and your defense mechanisms. You can't express anything until it goes through the Ascendant first. It reveals how you react to things, people, and ideas. Find the planet associated with the sign on your Ascendant. This is called your chart ruler, and it's the star of your chart. Being "ruler" of a sign means that the ruling planet and its energies are the primary influence.

CAN MY SIGNS CHANGE? Every few years it seems people get all upset that their horoscope has shifted and now they are an entirely different sign. Well, that's only half true. There are actually two different types of astrology. Tropical and sidereal. In this book, and in most Western-practicing astrology, we use tropical. But there's a whole other system of astrology that is based on where the stars are, not where the earth's axis is—which by the way has indeed moved ever so slightly. Sidereal basically defines the constellations based on fixed stars while tropical bases the constellations on the ecliptic. In other words, sidereal astrology is concerned with outer space only, while tropical is based on our perspective from earth. Like the different house systems, both work.

FIRST
QUADRANT

We are now going to start our journey around the Astrology Wheel. Our first step will be to take a look at which sign is on the cusp of each house. This will be the sign that rules that house for you.

Planets and aspects and other elements add even more richness, but we're going to do one rotation around the Zodiac primarily considering the houses and signs before we go further and really examine the significance of the planets.

In this section, I will also give you an example of a famous person who had a strong showing in that particular house and reveal some ways that the zodiac manifests in your own life. Finally, I leave you with a question to ponder as you consider the zodiac signs associated with each of your houses.

EMPTY HOUSES   Do you see an empty house or multiple empty houses! Not to fear, that doesn't mean you are in any way deficient. It simply means you aren't working as hard on that area in this lifetime. We'll go over empty houses and their significance in much greater detail in Chapter Seven.

The Astrology Wheel is broken up into four sections called quadrants. Each quadrant contains three houses, and they are called the Angular House, the Succedent House, and the Cadent House, in that order. The Angular Houses are the First, Fourth, Seventh, and Tenth houses, which correspond to the cardinal signs of Aries, Cancer, Libra, and Capricorn. If the astrological chart you're reading shows a lot of planets in these three houses, the chart's energy has a significant cardinal influence. These cardinal signs are often the pushier and more action-oriented signs.

The Succedent Houses are the way we astrologers classify the Second, Fifth, Eighth, and Eleventh Houses. They correlate to the fixed signs of Taurus, Leo, Scorpio, and Aquarius—a group of stubborn yet practical and grounded signs (so if you see a lot of your planets in these houses take note of that influence). Cadent Houses are associated with the Third, Sixth, Ninth, and Twelfth houses and the signs of Gemini, Virgo, Sagittarius, and Pisces. These are the mutable signs, and if you see a lot of planets in these places, there's often a more free-spirited, easygoing, and flexible undercurrent to the person.

THE ANGULAR HOUSES: The First, Fourth, Seventh, and Tenth houses, corresponding to Aries, Cancer, Libra, and Capricorn.

THE SUCCEDENT HOUSES: The Second, Fifth, Eighth, and Eleventh houses, corresponding to Taurus, Leo, Scorpio, and Aquarius.

THE CADENT HOUSES: The Third, Sixth, Ninth, and Twelfth houses, corresponding to Gemini, Virgo, Sagittarius, and Pisces.

We're going to start at the first quadrant, which is all about the self.

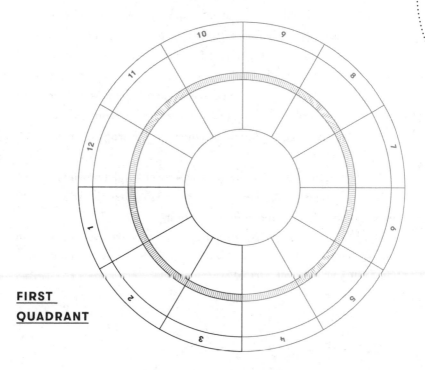

FIRST QUADRANT

The quadrants move counterclockwise from the beginning of self-actualization to the integrated self in society. I like to view the lower half of the wheel as "ME," and the upper half as "WE."

If you have lots of planets in this First Quadrant, this lifetime is focused on the discovery of your own identity and your own true self-worth. Interacting with others only furthers your progress into the big, beautiful exploration of yourself!

Check and see if your natal chart has a stellium (more than three planets and possibly a Sun or Moon in the same house). If the answer is yes, then it usually ends up creating a heavy concentration of a specific type of energy for you. The stellium might manifest itself in your life as a trial to overcome or as a gentle shepherd. In fact, a stellium is so powerful that it can actually subdue your Sun sign—if your Sun sign is not involved in your stellium. For example: If you have a stellium in Scorpio but you were born with your Sun in Gemini, you may find that you're a lot more introverted, emotional, and fascinated by life's darkness than your average Gemini.

So here in this First Quadrant we can sort of boil it down to saying here's where you'll get information on your ego (First House), money/things (Second House), and communication.

The First Quadrant is a thrilling place to start your journey. It is the place of self-identity, and we begin with the Ascendant (First House) where we uncover YOU.

FIRST HOUSE
AKA HOUSE OF SELF

RELATED SIGN AND PLANET: Aries and Mars

AREAS OF INFLUENCE: Early Life, Self-Image, and Persona

POSITIVE ATTRIBUTE: Self-knowledge

NEGATIVE ATTRIBUTE: Acting too selfish

HOW TO BALANCE: Learning to love yourself for who you are

The First House is where it all begins. Check to see which zodiac sign is on the cusp. Make a note of it, because that little sucker is your Ascendant, aka your Rising Sign, which is simply the constellation that was on the eastern horizon at the exact moment of your birth.

First impressions matter, and as such the Ascendant is hands down one of the most important factors in your chart. It is what people see when they first meet you. It's the face and energy that you project into the world, and while it may be very similar to who you are, it could also be wildly different from your real self. That all depends on your chart as a whole!

I like to think of the Ascendant as more of a mask that we wear. The side of you that you put out there to absolute strangers when you go to a party, a business conference, a new book club. Once people really get to know you, they'll see more than your First House.

This First House also denotes your physical appearance, your looks, your vitality, your health, and the way you'd like others to see you. It represents your first breath of life, fresh starts, new beginnings, and your first impressions. Any planet(s) that you have in this realm will play into your personality. Planets add extra flair and purpose to your First House and their influence cannot be hidden! In fact, any planet in the First House is extremely visible in contrast to the hidden Twelfth House, where everything is oh so subtle and hard to see . . . but more on that later.

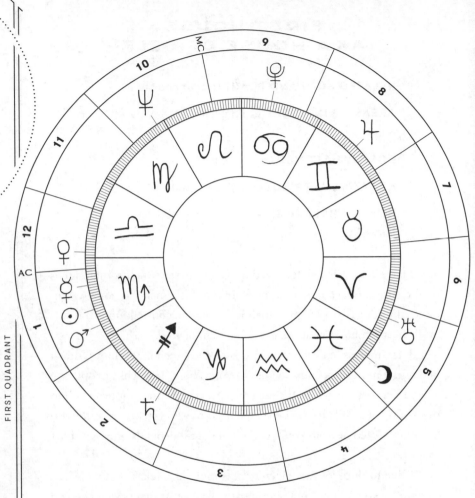

Let's take a look at the chart of Grace Kelly, brilliant actress and later Princess of Monaco. She had a loaded First House with Mercury, Sun, and Mars all in Scorpio. This means it was her divine calling to be a true shining individualist with amazing leadership abilities. Well, she was a princess after all! Also, a great mother with a charitable heart thanks to her Pisces Moon. It's quite a feat to have so much in the First House. One can easily become too self-absorbed, using one's powerful persona for ill instead of good. But Grace was one smart cookie. She flung herself into stage acting and then later leveraged her sunny personality to raise heaps of money for orphanages and hospitals. It also helps that energetic Mars is so close to her Sun, and Venus and

Mercury near her Ascendant. People saw grace (no pun intended) and beauty, but also a fiery and intelligent spirit.

So what do you have?

The First House in Aries

If your Ascendant is in the sign of Aries, it's going to be super important to know your limits, when to unleash your energy and when to keep it nice and contained. One challenge will be that you can sometimes have a hard time caring for others, or accepting that care for yourself. It's going to take work to mind compassion for your own emotional needs, and for other people's.

The First House in Taurus

If your chart begins in Taurus, you are all about those hedonistic earthly pleasures. While that's obviously a whole lot of fun, you might need to watch out for weight gain or dipping into self-destructive behavior. Once you can accept life's changes, and the fact that change is a necessary—and often beautiful—part of our journey here on earth, you can find true liberation.

The First House in Gemini

If your Ascendant is in Gemini you're going to be the kind of person who wants to keep moving, trying new things, talking to everyone. (Did I say keep moving, phew, you are really on the go!) Folks born with this Rising Sign are often on the thin side (all that energy) and they are definitely the kind of person you want on your brainstorm team. Careful to keep your focus, it can be a real challenge.

The First House in Cancer

When your First House begins in the sign of Cancer, you, my dear, are ruled by your many moods. You're a fabulous nurturer, though! Don't be surprised if people flock to you with their problems. Just be careful you don't let an opportunity pass you by because you didn't feel like it.

The First House in Leo

With your First House set in the sign of Leo, you have a massive amount of presence right off the bat! You have the cojones to be brave in the most challenging of situations. Your issue to work on is to not let your image of yourself bog you down. You don't have to be the biggest and bestest at everything all the time. Your work will be to focus on what makes you tick as an individual and, better yet, get out of your own head and think about how you can contribute to the betterment of humanity.

The First House in Virgo

If your Ascendant is in Virgo then you were born to help others. You might have some health issues but you rock in the areas of intelligence and clarity of thought (you're like the Marie Kondo of the mind). The biggest challenge for you is to see the forest, not just the trees. And while trust is good, be sure to add a grain of salt in your dealings with some people.

The First House in Libra

If your First House is in the sign of Libra, you get your energy from those around you, which can sometimes unbalance you and lead to exhaustion. Accept constructive criticism and be open to physical activities to thrive under this beautiful Ascendant.

The First House in Scorpio

When you're born with Scorpio Ascendant, you radiate a certain internal power, and often attract others with your sensitivity. While you put the capital I in intense, sometimes you need to back off the emo. Not every feel needs to be felt quite so intensely. And if you wanted to forgive and forget after experiencing a slight, it would do your body good.

The First House in Sagittarius

If you're born with your Ascendant in Sagittarius then you might just have a calling as a teacher, or enjoy dabbling in philosophy. You're the life of a party, and people take genuine pleasure being in your orbit. Just make sure to take a breath when you need to solve a problem, think it through, and look for a straightforward, practical solution.

The First House in Capricorn

If your Ascendant is in the sign of Capricorn, you're born with a to-do list, and boy do you love checking items off of it. You might struggle to empathize with those you deem weak, or simply not as strong and efficient as yourself. Once you make peace with your own inferiorities, you'll grow compassion for everyone else.

The First House in Aquarius

If your Ascendant is in Aquarius, you were born to stand out in a crowd. Rebel, rebel, you've got your hands full in this life learning to peel back your layers and figure out what eccentric, glorious creature exists in the core of your being. And while you're doing that, remember to respect yourself and others.

The First House in Pisces

If your First House begins in the sign of Pisces, you're on a mission in this life, looking to serve in the duty to a higher cause than yourself. You're also highly creative, dreamy, and sneaky! You guys make fabulous actors, but be careful with whom you surround yourself. You're a natural at soaking up energy—the good and the bad.

DIG DEEPER

Some astrologers refer to your Rising Sign as your mask. Think about why and how you may be presenting a different face to the world from what you truly feel inside. Consider ways you can seek to reconcile these two images of yourself.

SECOND HOUSE
AKA HOUSE OF VALUES

RELATED SIGN AND PLANET: Taurus and Venus

AREAS OF INFLUENCE: Who and what you value, including yourself and your possessions

POSITIVE ATTRIBUTES: Noble values and fabulous taste

NEGATIVE ATTRIBUTES: Reckless spending and low self-esteem

HOW TO BALANCE: Finding stability and security in your own self-worth

The Second House is also known as the Money House, but it will serve you better to think of this as the house of wealth/abundance since it reveals how you view your possessions, how you spend your money, and how you tend to attract it. It's the house that denotes what you hold dear. If you've got a strong Second House, you're definitely here to make the green stuff, but there's a catch! Ultimately, it's what you do with the green stuff that *really* matters. So while this house does, in fact, denote if you are a money magnet or a frugal spender, it's your basic financial principles that really count. Values, folks. It's crucial to our human development.

While the Second House can reveal a lot about our income, the way we spend our resources uncovers much more about our true identity. After all, it's in this house that we begin to learn what it is we need for our very own safety and security. An imperative thing, right? Right. It's those instilled values that really bring your self-worth into focus. You just can't be a top-notch individual without the added benefit of some good ol' fashioned integrity. It's the underlying secret of the Second House.

Are you a Scrooge or a philanthropist? Well, that depends on the sign, planets, and aspects that inhabit your money realm. Let's take a peek at Elvis Presley.

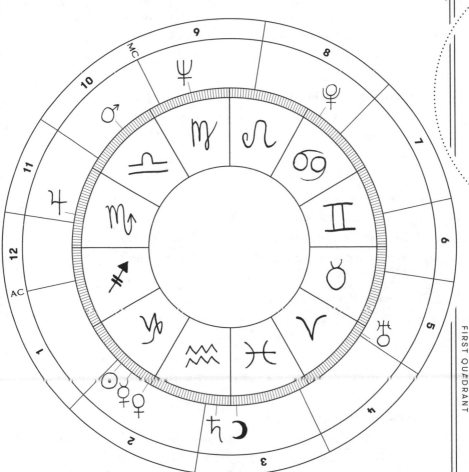

The King has a strong Second House with his Capricorn Sun, Mercury, and Venus showing up there. (By the way, if you're lucky enough to have Venus or Jupiter here, you naturally lure money into your life—though holding on to it is an entirely different story!) Elvis has Capricorn on the cusp of his Money House, so this makes Saturn the ruler of his Second House. And Elvis has Saturn beautifully placed in his Third, the House of Communication. Yep, Elvis made his money with his voice. But Elvis also overspent, overindulged, and overdid everything. All very Second House conundrums. He was tacky thanks to his Venus opposite Pluto and squared by Uranus. But despite his gaudy, rhinestone style, Elvis was actually quite charitable with his money.

Your turn! Take a look at your chart and notice what planets are showing up for you. If you need to, refer back to the glyphs on pages 20–21 for reference.

The Second House in Aries

Do you spy an Aries located in the cusp of your Second House? Congratulations! This often signals that you're the kind of person with a natural instinct for success in the material world. One piece of advice, though, if I might? Slow down. Chew your food, spice meals with care, and take time to smell the roses. And maybe check to see where your Moon is located (more on that in Chapter 15). With any luck, it, or one of the more feminine energy planets like Venus, Neptune, or Pluto, are positioned in places that smooth out your rough edges.

The Second House in Taurus

Gotta Second House in Taurus? Lucky you, as this is a great position for this house in terms of earning the green stuff. You're meant to enjoy material success, so go on and treat yourself. Just make sure you don't let yourself feel guilty about it—that will spoil everything.

The Second House in Gemini

Is Gemini kicking it in your Second House? Then, distinguished guests, we have a side hustler on our hands. You have an affinity with the gig economy, which can be full of fun and flexibility . . . just so long as you don't get into shady dealings. Keep it on the up-and-up to find harmony.

The Second House in Cancer

If you're a person whose Second House begins in the sign of Cancer, then we don't need to consult a Magic 8-Ball to know that your outlook is "pretty damn good" that you're going to either go into the family business or strike out on your own. Remote work from a home office might suit you just fine. Also notice how you might hold on to money, tending to only want to spend it on home or family.

The Second House in Leo

If your Second House's cusp is in the sign of Leo, you use the stage to make your money. And that doesn't necessarily mean Broadway! Wherever you work, you find a way to be front and center, the presentation person on a team, or the "Show me the money" one in sports. Wherever you work, you're passionate and sometimes a little theatrical, but always oh so so confident. Make sure that your ego is able to be held in check because sometimes feedback is valuable. Your self-worth and ego shouldn't be measured by anyone but yourself, so don't give up your power to colleagues.

The Second House in Virgo

If your Second House's cusp is in the sign of Virgo, you need to learn when to rest on your laurels. If you're a fan of the musical *Hamilton*, you've got something in common with the show's namesake: Neither of you is ever satisfied. You aren't likely to win the lottery or make a killing in an MLM, but if you work hard and use your keen eye for detail, you're going to be just fine.

The Second House in Libra

When your Second House is set in the sign of Libra, you're the kind of person who loves to be on a team, and also have an issue tying your self-worth through external relationships with other people. You might choose a spouse who has the ability to provide, but don't let that make you jealous . . . or worse yet, greedy. You're going to be happiest when you can work with others.

The Second House in Scorpio

Does your Second House have Scorpio on the cusp? Okay, a lot of your financial success in this life might hinge on members of your family who came before you. If anyone stands a chance to have inherited a fortune, or a debt, it's you. You are going to be happiest when you let go of control and accept the flow of your circumstances.

The Second House in Sagittarius

So, you're a person who has a Second House with its cusp in the sign of Sagittarius? I'm not saying you waste money, but, ahem, you might find it dang easy to burn through it. You are going to go out hard, spend big, and have way too much fun. But darling, there is wisdom in moderation. Try to be realistic about how you show up, what you demand to be paid, and remember there's no shame in working your way up from the ground floor. We can't all start in the corner office.

The Second House in Capricorn

Have a Capricorn on the cusp of your Second House? You're another one of those "work hard for what you get" types, and there's no shame in that game. You deserve what you earn, and that will make you content, as long as you don't drift into hoarding and greed. You're better off to learn the lesson of sharing your wealth to really find core satisfaction.

The Second House in Aquarius

Does your Second House begin in the sign of Aquarius? Well, risks don't worry you, baby. Neither does innovation. You see solutions nobody else would ever dream of and while money doesn't matter as much to you, you often attract success by pulling off seemingly impossible schemes.

The Second House in Pisces

With your Second House at the cusp of Pisces, people are often going to hear you say "Hey, where are my keys?" "Um, has anybody seen my wallet?" You might be overconfident in your ability to make investments so if you have a trusted friend or family member who is adept at money management, you'd be best off listening to their advice.

DIG DEEPER

Find your journal or a piece of paper and jot down
some tangible things that you value. Now list some
intangible things. Great job! Now reflect on why these
items are important to you. What does this say about
what you value?

THIRD HOUSE
AKA HOUSE OF COMMUNICATION

RELATED SIGN AND PLANET: Gemini and Mercury

AREAS OF INFLUENCE: Learning, teaching, conversation, information

POSITIVE ATTRIBUTES: Eloquent with words and honesty

NEGATIVE ATTRIBUTES: Gossip, secrets, manipulative information

HOW TO BALANCE: Speaking your truth without fear

The Third House is also known as the Communication Realm. This is the place where we gather information, process it, and speak it aloud. It rules short trips, running errands, chatting with your neighbors, texting your friends. It also reveals your relationships with your siblings, if you have them.

This is the house that rules our intellect and our mind. It reveals how we process and analyze facts and info and how we, in turn, convey that knowledge to others. Hence teaching, speaking, sales, public relations, marketing, acting, writing, even singing all fall under the Third House. Strong Third House people are usually intelligent with agile minds. They tend to process things quickly. Absorbing information at lightning speed and always wanting more. This is the key to a healthy Third House: Idle minds are a dangerous thing here. Keep that mind active and busy, and never ever stop accessing information.

The Communication Realm also shows what our education was like pre-college. But the clever among us, even without the benefit of a good education, can twist their lack of book learning into their favor. Crafty folks often have quite a few planets in their Third House. It's up to you, however, whether you use your information for enlightenment or for calculated gossip.

Let's look at the chart of bestselling horror author Stephen King.

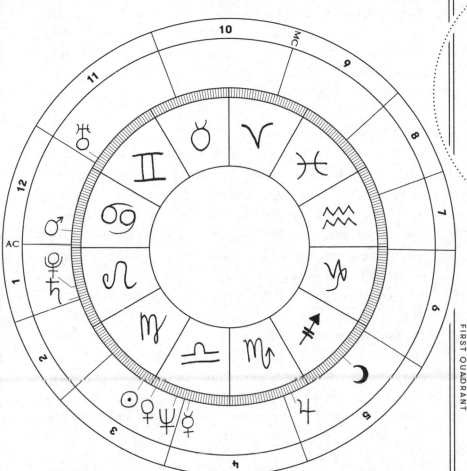

Now here's a brilliant soul with his Sun, Venus, and Neptune all occupying his Third House. He has detailed and analytical Virgo on the cusp of his Communication Realm, granting him diligence, efficiency, and strong mental agility. And the ruler of his Third House is Mercury, opposite his Midheaven or career cusp, so it's unsurprising that words are what he is famous for. And just for fun let's look at his Money House, ruled by Leo. This means the Sun is his financial ruler, which is beautifully located in his Communication Realm.

But it's Stephen's Venus and Neptune that reveal more about his Third House. No way could he succeed by being a salesman, or as a marketing manager, with the planet of inspiration and imagination here. He has to fabricate and beautify his words with Venus and Neptune. Fiction is the only way to do it. Singing could work too. Otherwise he could use that energy in a sneaky way. Like being not-so-honest when it comes to selling a car. But Stephen is smart and he crafted a very successful Third House.

The Third House in Aries

If your Third House has the sign of Aries at the cusp, you might be a bit of a bulldozer. Blame it on your lightning-quick mind and incredible energy, but this is bound to get you into trouble. Watch that temper and try to be aware of group dynamics and know when you're starting to dominate a leeeetle too much. If you dislike someone, they're probably going to know it—diplomatic tact isn't something you're amazing at, but if you're communicating with a person you respect, and who can keep up with you, you're likely going to find happiness.

The Third House in Taurus

Having Taurus at the cusp of your Third House means you don't mind spreadsheets or doing your taxes. There's a good chance that you're a visual learner and that you function best with an organized inbox and digital folders. Your challenges are going to revolve around your lack of flexibility and your dislike of chance.

The Third House in Gemini

Gemini in your Third House? Well, that's a lovely thing to see. If you've got siblings you are likely close to them, and if not, it may be worthwhile to work on those relationships—they are tied to your true happiness. You're not going to exaggerate or tell a lie, but you might find it difficult to make yourself emotionally vulnerable. Because you're such a quick learner and communicator, try to position yourself in roles where you need to have interpersonal communication skills; you'd also make the grade as a teacher.

The Third House in Cancer

If your Third House is in Cancer, look to your family, as you often inherit your intelligence from them. Hopefully they are educated and articulate, but if not, have some sympathy because your lack of access to education is likely systemic. You may have a reputation for locking yourself in a glass house of emotions, muddling the rational with the emotional. Find a way to express your emotions in a healthy way that others can hear, and you're going to be on the right track.

The Third House in Leo

When the Third House cusp is in the sign of Leo, you think about yourself a lot. Like . . . a lot a lot. This is awesome if you are well aware of your ego and don't take things personally. But if you struggle with codependency, or find it difficult to take constructive criticism, this is an area where you will feel stress. Remember to love your inner child and take time to accept yourself warts and all.

The Third House in Virgo

Got your Third House set in Virgo? Hmmmmmm this is interesting, very interesting. On the one hand you are able to speak with intelligence and remarkable clarity, but on the other hand sometimes you channel this into all-nighters on WebMD trying to figure out a diagnosis for something that ails you. While health troubles can crop up in this arrangement, it's also quite likely hypochondria. Those Virgo Third Housers know all the yucky things to catch and all the subsequent symptoms. If you stop turning your attention to your body mechanics (and their faults) you have the potential to let go of the bad stuff to receive the good stuff.

The Third House in Libra

If your Third House is set in the sign of Libra, you might love you some reality television. Wow, you just love to dissect other people's lives and gossip is your jam. You also are a champion of the underdogs and you're at your best when you can lift others up.

The Third House in Scorpio

When your Third House starts in Scorpio, you can be a lot to handle. Sure, you're funny in a biting, often dark sort of way, but you can also be a bit of a complainer, always looking at the glass half empty. Do you catch yourself saying "Why does this always happen to me?" a lot. Yeah, thought so, sweetie. But never fear, if you put in the work (through therapy and self-care) in focusing on the positive good things in life, you could experience powerful transformations.

The Third House in Sagittarius

Those with the Third House in Sagittarius have the gift of gab. You are a great one for waxing philosophical and getting into debates, although usually you argue from a place of sunny optimism. This is a position for philosophical thinkers and people of wide perspectives, opinions that always shift to more positive views. You're also voted Most Likely to Get Lost Driving in Your Own Town, and please don't use your phone while driving. You are scattered enough. Take the time to focus, and maybe pop on a lighthearted nonfiction audiobook. You do just love to learn new things.

The Third House in Capricorn

With that Third House starting in Capricorn, you're one tough nut. Capricorn is normally all about the rational and practical, but here in the Third House you might be smacking up against some karma or prior damage. Give yourself some grace, remember that rest is your friend, and use your stubbornness to maintain good boundaries. If all else fails, call it a day and go to bed. The world will always look better to you in the morning.

WHAT IS KARMA? Spiritual "cause and effect." The actions and deeds of this life, and past lives, which can influence a person's future.

The Third House in Aquarius

If Aquarius lands at the cusp of your Third House, I know these things in an instant: You're a rebel who is fiercely independent, you're brilliant, and you might be a bit of a know-it-all. Guess what, you also might make an excellent astrologer! You also need to take good care of that body, because it's a temple for your fantastic mind.

The Third House in Pisces

Okay, so you have Pisces at the cusp to your Third House. I've got some good news and bad news. There can be a lot of emotional conflict with this placement, and a frustration in getting your point across. Take a gander at where your Mercury, Jupiter, and Neptune are in the natal chart because they might be in grounding areas. Since clarity can be a challenge, it's not recommended that you indulge in mind-altering substances, so don't go on that ayahuasca trip with your besties—mkay?

PUTTING IT
ALL TOGETHER

Do you see a lot of planets in this First Quadrant? If the answer is yes, your life journey may call for a lot of self-reflection, and you might be on a mission to improve your communication with others.

You are the kind of person who is likely going to benefit from spending more time alone to stay in touch with your own identity and tune in to your own needs and wants. Please work to stay grounded, because you are not well suited to losing yourself in others.

Remember it's okay if a person has an opinion different from yours. Consider listening to their POV rather than jumping in to give your two cents. The more variety of people you interact with, the richer your life will be.

The universe wants you to lean into yourself, get in touch with what you value, and what fosters a strong sense of self-worth.

DIG DEEPER

How do you communicate to those who are most precious to you? Are you able to share your deepest needs and desires? Why or why not?

SECOND QUADRANT

4

The Second Quadrant of the Astrology Wheel includes the Fourth, Fifth, and Sixth Houses, and where the First Quadrant was focused primarily on ourselves, the Second Quadrant delves more into our awareness of others. The Second Quadrant deals with family, children, and work relationships. So this means if you have heaps of planets in this particular quadrant, you're learning how to assimilate your identity in relation to others.

FOURTH HOUSE
AKA HOUSE OF HOME & FAMILY

RELATED SIGN AND PLANET: Cancer and Moon

AREAS OF INFLUENCE: Your roots, your tribe, your home

POSITIVE ATTRIBUTE: Creating a peaceful and safe sanctuary

NEGATIVE ATTRIBUTE: Trapped in outdated traditions determined by your parents

HOW TO BALANCE: Learning to trust your intuition

The Fourth House is located at the very bottom of your chart. It denotes your family, your roots, your foundations, and it's associated with the mothering and nurturing sign of Cancer. This is the house that reveals what life was like when you were young, and what you'll be like in your old age. It usually shows one of your parents too, but astrologers differ on whether it's your mom or your dad (although the majority say dad).

The homey fourth sector of your chart is where you go to get away from it all. It's your safe place and it reveals what makes you comfy and secure. It's not just your physical home either! Learning how to align with the comfort and security of your *inner self* is an imperative lesson for many with a strong Fourth House. This is also a very psychic house, as it pulls in intuition and discloses a need to understand the very basis of human behavior. Lots of people with strong Fourth Houses are highly gifted with fabulous gut instincts and incredible insight. These are also the souls who love to stay up late at night. After all, if your Sun is here, you were born close to midnight!

In a more literal expression of home, real estate is also highly linked to this house. And you can tell a lot about what sort of home appeals to someone by merely glimpsing their Fourth House. For instance, if someone has Pisces or Neptune there, they'll feel more comfortable near water. Gemini on the cusp of the Fourth House can indicate someone who likes a lot of people and lively conversation in their home.

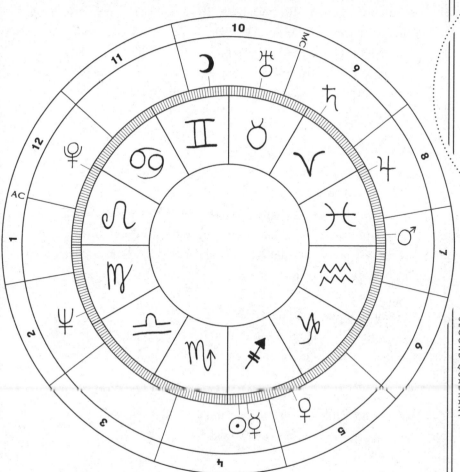

Take a look at the chart of rock-star legend Tina Turner. Underneath that dynamic and showy Leo Rising and Sag Sun is a very private individual. Tina has her Sun and Mercury both in the Fourth House, indicating a deeply sensitive and secluded homebody. And with secretive Scorpio on the Fourth House cusp, she definitely wants a more quiet and remote hideaway. Something you would never know with wild Uranus at the top of her chart!

The Fourth House in Aries

If you find your Fourth House cusp set in the sign of Aries, you might have mommy issues if you identify as a man, or daddy issues if you identify as a woman. It's not always the case but you may also have pain—even some sort of abuse—that runs deep in your family. Your childhood home might have been loud or full of fighting (fiery debates or angry conflicts). No matter what, though, you're a provider and as you look forward in this life, you're going to make the people under you feel protected.

The Fourth House in Taurus

Here in the Fourth House set in Taurus, we see people who grew up as the apple of their parents' eye. There's a good chance that you weren't the kid who had to eat alone in the lunch room or was chosen last for a school project. This is quite a healthy and warm person who might have more traditional values than some, but has a real sense of comfort and stability in their lives.

The Fourth House in Gemini

With your Fourth House cusp in Gemini, there might have been some real inconsistencies or falsehoods in your childhood. You might be the sort of person who gravitates more to a chosen family, rather than a family of origin for deep emotional investment. You're also the type of person who, while inclined to ask family for advice, even when you get it you're going to do what you want anyway.

The Fourth House in Cancer

With your Fourth House set in Cancer you've got a strong connection to the idea of family. In fact, you might well be interested in genealogy or other ways you can connect to your ancestors. I'm going to go ahead and vote you Most Likely to Take a DNA Test to Learn Your Family Origins.

The Fourth House in Leo

With that Fourth House kicking off in the sign of Leo, your home often reflects its VIP—you! You're going to be the one who takes guests around to look at your new renovations or the amazing chicken coop you built out back by the garden. You might have had a parent that hogged the limelight and didn't leave you with much space or encouragement to develop emotionally healthy practices. Looking to religious or spiritual outlets will prove grounding.

The Fourth House in Virgo

Hey, you've got a Fourth House cusp in Virgo and you know what that means! (Or, actually, you don't, which is why you're reading this, but still!) There is something out of whack in your home. Maybe it was not receiving unconditional love. Maybe it was never hearing a "Well done, honey" when you made the grade. You weren't born damaged but sometimes you might have been made to feel that way. As a result, you're often looking to re-create that "perfect" idea of home that you never had. Perfection is an illusion, and honestly, honey, give yourself a break. You're doing great.

The Fourth House in Libra

If your Fourth House is set in Libra, you idealize your parents' relationship. You also might feel like you shouldn't mess with perfection and aim to build your own family in a similar way. You're going to look to your parents to influence what you want in your own life as an adult.

The Fourth House in Scorpio

Ah, there's that Fourth House in Scorpio. Here's a sign that takes those darkest, deepest emotions, ones we all try to pretend don't exist—and you stuff that ish deep. My challenge for you is to pull out those painful, yucky memories, forgive them, and let go. They don't serve you and you were put here on this planet to smile. When you find the person that gives you this reason, you're never going to want to let them go.

The Fourth House in Sagittarius

If your Fourth House is in Sagittarius, home is where the heart is; the issue for your restless spirit is that home might need to be somewhere else, far far away, even another country. Once you have space and distance, you can often look back on what worked or didn't in your childhood. You're going to be happiest when you find your place, even if it's in an unexpected location.

The Fourth House in Capricorn

Okay, take a deep breath, friend—having the Fourth House in Capricorn can be hard. You might believe in a higher power and use that as a lodestar. You want to correct the mistakes done by your parents, and while that's admirable, it's exhausting. The good news is that you create a much more stable and loving and emotionally healthy relationship for the people in the home you create. It's a lot of work, but it does tend to pay off.

The Fourth House in Aquarius

So with your Fourth House in Aquarius, you might have moved around a lot as a kid or experienced parental divorce at a highly sensitive juncture in your childhood. Freedom is the sweetest word to you, more so even than "home" (don't tell the Cancers, they just won't understand). As a result, it takes you longer than most to happily settle down. Sow your wild oats while you can, and when you *do* commit to building a home it's likely going to be full of the latest and greatest Apple products and with a significant other who you consider a very best friend.

The Fourth House in Pisces

Ooooooh, you have Pisces in your Fourth House. This might point to some shady folks in your family tree. That's exciting! Less exciting is that it could be you didn't receive clear and constant emotion as a youngster. This might have left a deep-seated feeling of being less than or not quite belonging to your family of birth. Addiction issues might plague relatives. Happily, when you do create a home you are probably going to be extra sentimental, creating elaborate scrapbooks and frequently setting a place at your table for guests.

DIG DEEPER

Look around your home. How is it serving you? What small changes could you make to feel more comfortable or connected in your personal environment?

FIFTH HOUSE
AKA HOUSE OF PLEASURE

RELATED SIGN AND PLANET: Leo and Sun

AREAS OF INFLUENCE: Romance, children, art, how you have fun

POSITIVE ATTRIBUTE: Tapping into your creative side

NEGATIVE ATTRIBUTES: Gambling and hedonism

HOW TO BALANCE: Fulfilling your artistic side without being childish

The Fifth House is associated with the creative, dramatic, and gifted sign of Leo, and if you've got a strong Fifth House that's pretty much what you're here to do. Be creative! Basically it's your job to show us all of your many talents so you can make the rest of us blissfully happy. Quite an order, eh? But Fifth House folks are natural entertainers, they shine and sparkle without even thinking about it!

This is the house that reveals what your inner child finds fun and exciting. Are you a crazed daredevil or a more stodgy and reserved type? It's the House of Pleasure, so any planets here help shape what sorts of things knock your socks off. The Fifth House also shows what sort of children you might have, if you choose to have them at all. Many Fifth House people also work comfortably with children, as they themselves are quite childlike. Just remember to apply that youthful side in a positive way and not in a *childish* way. Romance governs this realm too, so how you received love as a child, and how you now return it, are revealed by the Fifth House. This can really show what you're like in your dating life, but remember that it's really the Seventh House that discloses what you are like in your committed relationships.

Gambling and risk taking linger here too, as does drama and theater. All things Leo! In general this is where you're spontaneous, artistic, and ready for a good time. Strong Fifth Housers run on imagination, creative endeavors, and charisma. It's almost impossible to stay mad at them for too long. They're way too much fun.

Take a look at Fifth House powerhouse Dolly Parton. She has Mercury, Venus, and Sun all in this realm and in the business-oriented sign of Capricorn. Dolly is a creative force and with both Mars and Saturn opposite her Fifth House planets her drive is unstoppable. Just having both her Sun and her chart ruler Mercury here automatically makes Dolly quite the artistic genius, but it's that Saturn opposition that keeps her going. She is always working to better herself, as it's hard for her to be satisfied. Which really just benefits the rest of us in the long run. And even though Dolly has a demure Virgo Rising, her iconic hair is *très* Leo, don't you think?

The Fifth House in Aries

With your Fifth House in Aries, you are going to want to get a lot of exercise. Invest in that CrossFit membership! Train for a marathon! You thrive on that endorphin rush. You are also on the hunt for self-love, and with your unflagging energy you are going to keep looking for what brings joy at your core until you find it.

The Fifth House in Taurus

If your Fifth House is the sign of Taurus, sensuality and pleasure go hand in hand. You might find yourself attracted to possessive or self-indulgent people, but yearn for sensual pleasures and uncomplicated romance. Art makes a fabulous hobby for you.

The Fifth House in Gemini

If your Fifth House is set to Gemini, you'll have a vibrant inner child. What is going to make you happiest is opportunities for rich and stimulating conversations. Host dinner parties. Rock out on Reddit. Engage with your fellow humans and keep on expressing yourself.

The Fifth House in Cancer

If your Fifth House is in the sign of Cancer, you will feel happiest when you're unleashing creativity and artistic flair. You're also going to be a happy homebody who loves game night or a Netflix binge snuggled on the couch with your people.

The Fifth House in Leo

When your Fifth House is in the sign of Leo you know what is going to bring you happiness and you want it, preferably now. What might look like mountains to others are bumps in the road to you. Avoid getting involved with those who share your line of work, as you might get too competitive with each other.

The Fifth House in Virgo

With the Fifth House in Virgo, your challenge is to tell yourself that you got this—and then believe it. It's easy for you to measure yourself and find your output lacking, but if you can write or work with your hands you'll find a lot of personal satisfaction.

The Fifth House in Libra

Those who have a Fifth House set in the sign of Libra are the rare birds who do not believe hell is other people. No way. No how. Heaven is other people. But only special people. You don't want to scroll Tinder for hours. You want monogamous relationships and someone who will go to lectures with you, take a yoga class, help you find that all-important balance.

The Fifth House in Scorpio

If you've got your Fifth House set in the sign of Scorpio, you can face the darkness and remain unbroken. You might keep connections with family and friends disowned or shut out by others. You're not going to settle for anything less than exactly what you want.

The Fifth House in Sagittarius

If your Fifth House is set in Sagittarius, variety is the spice of life. You want to try new things (often in the bedroom) and go to exciting new places. New is good in your worldview, and you want to try everything life has to offer. Why not order a new sex toy? Right now. And splurge on a really nice high-end one. You know you won't regret it. . . .

The Fifth House in Capricorn

If your Fifth House is in the sign of Capricorn, you might enjoy pursuing creative projects, but you execute them in a logical manner. You might derive a lot of joy from historical research or even dabbling in the field of archaeology. If this hasn't been your "thing," try it and you might surprise yourself. At the very least watch *Indiana Jones*, because Harrison Ford is just so yum in khaki and cracking that whip.

The Fifth House in Aquarius

When Aquarius is in the Fifth House cusp you dream, and you dream big. The same old, same old is the kiss of death for you. What are you waiting for? Plant your flagpole. Leave your mark. If you have children, you're going to make them the center of your world. And they are also going to be the kids who go to school with purple hair and polyester princess dresses and rubber rainboots because they are expressing their individuality. And all you can do is say "hell yeah."

The Fifth House in Pisces

If the Fifth House begins in Pisces, you love that creative life, it's just that you're so intensely secretive with it. Do you know what? I want you to close this book and get out your art or your poetry or your photography or whatever you make that is so fabulous and find a way to share it. Post it online. Go to an open mic night. Take an improv class. Have an art show. It'll be scary. And it'll be worth it.

DIG DEEPER

What role does creativity play in your life? Are you satisfied with this answer, why or why not? Reflect on a special love affair, what made it important? What did it give you that you wish you could recapture in this present moment? How are you taking time to indulge yourself sensually and playfully?

SIXTH HOUSE
AKA HOUSE OF HEALTH

RELATED SIGN AND PLANET: Virgo and Mercury

AREAS OF INFLUENCE: Everyday work, service, and health

POSITIVE ATTRIBUTES: Adapting a strong health and work regime

NEGATIVE ATTRIBUTES: Unorganized and scattered

HOW TO BALANCE: Learning how to work smarter, not harder

The Sixth House is the realm of all things Virgo and it expresses your work ethic, your routines, schedules, and how you take care of yourself and your pets. How you perform on a daily basis is shown through this house. You'll find workaholics and people in service with a strong Sixth House, but they are not work addicts for fame's sake alone. Strong Sixth Housers are true, unequivocal, busy bees who would rather die than do a measly half-assed job. Yep. These are the true perfectionists. Every fiber of their being needs to do a good job. They simply won't stand for anything else.

Cleanliness is next to godliness with this house. How you organize your closet, your office, your pantry. It's all here in this house. As are your pets and your coworkers. This is the house that exposes your daily habits, and that includes brushing your teeth and feeding your calico cat. Health nuts fall into this area too, and you can glean quite a bit of info of how you were raised to take care of yourself in this house. What sort of exercise is best for you is found here as well as what sorts of food you find comforting. All of this may seem completely unglamorous, but this is actually a truly important house! And anyone who knows the feeling of a job well done can attest to the importance of that simple feeling.

Just like the sign of Virgo, the Sixth House is a meticulous place. It's where we scrutinize and demand order, or lack of, depending on your chart. It's where we overanalyze and where we get neurotic. The

Sixth House shows how we want to improve the world, and the hard work we need to do to accomplish it.

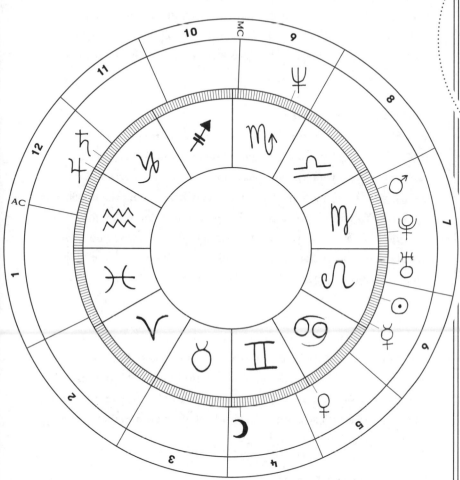

Let's look at the chart of former president Barack Obama. Barack has both Sun and Mercury in the Sixth House and in the royal sign of Leo. Here is a man with high ideals who truly wants to make the world a better place, and his Mercury is opposite Jupiter for amazing optimism. Here is a hard worker who demands the best in all that he does. And even though he is a Leo, it's truly not fame that he is after, but a deep sense of service and altruism.

The Sixth House in Aries

When your Sixth House is in your Aries cusp, you are a kind and dedicated hard worker—you might take particular joy in getting a fancy planner or taking up bullet journaling. Make sure that you know your value, and be skeptical of those who want to volunteer your skills. You are also the kind of person who finds a great deal of joy and satisfaction in creating your own business.

The Sixth House in Taurus

When you've got a Sixth House in Taurus, you might work hard, but you better believe you are going to play hard too. When you're on the clock, you give it your all, but you're not going to be a person who wants their boss contacting them after hours or when getting slacked on the weekend. You aren't going to be happy doing a mere day job. When you show up to work, you need to be happy, otherwise you're going to risk being the person who calls in sick or sneaks games of Solitaire when no one's looking.

The Sixth House in Gemini

So your Sixth House is in Gemini, is it? Then every day better look different for you, and you're going to shine when you're in charge of putting out a lot of little fires as opposed to working in fields that have you waiting years for results. While you are usually friendly and talkative, set boundaries, otherwise those around you might dump their problems on your lap and drain your energy.

The Sixth House in Cancer

Okay, your House of Health is in the sign of Cancer. This means that you might be the sort who takes their work home with you. I don't mean this in terms of working late on a project, more like you are going to stew over stressful encounters. Your worst nightmare is if your boss says "Hey, can we schedule a meeting tomorrow" with no context. Also, when you get home, pour your favorite beverage, turn on some music, and put down your devices. Allow yourself a moment to breathe deep and disconnect from the day's hubbub.

The Sixth House in Leo

Ya'll with Leo at the cusp of your Sixth House in Leo want to have lots of fun when you work and even more importantly, you want to be praised. If there's an Employee of the Month program at your workplace, you're gunning for it. That's great, but it can leave you physically and mentally vulnerable to stress if you aren't getting that regular positive reinforcement.

The Sixth House in Virgo

If Virgo is the ruler of your Sixth House astrology, it feels right at home here. You're going to be a highly analytical, focused, and hardworking person who is very invested in their profession. You might feel particularly satisfied if your job has a strong helping component such as education, social work, or medicine. Watch your stress levels carefully, and if you get out of balance you might find yourself reaching for the antacids, as your stomach is usually the canary in your body's coal mine. In times of stress, such people may experience problems with digestion.

The Sixth House in Libra

It's no big surprise that those whose Sixth House is in Libra want to strike a good balance between work and home. You might well love your job, but you know you aren't your profession, and so you place just as much value on the time you have outside of work. You might be well suited to a career in family law, conflict resolution, or customer service.

The Sixth House in Scorpio

If your Sixth House's cusp is in Scorpio, you might find work to be something of an obsession. Freelancing is likely going to be an area that brings you joy, just as long as there is plenty of creativity and a low amount of routine.

The Sixth House in Sagittarius

Got Sagittarius in your Sixth House? Well, people just love working with you. The problem is that if you get bored, you're likely to be the office distraction, sending out Slack DMs or trying to entice others into long Gchats. But if you find value in the work you do, you pour your heart and soul into the role.

The Sixth House in Capricorn

If you have your Sixth House in Capricorn, you love color coding your calendar and crafting to-do lists. You are a workhorse and may find yourself sticking around a workplace while others leave for greener pastures. Make sure that you enjoy what you do and that you're not stuck in a routine.

The Sixth House in Aquarius

If Aquarius is in your Sixth House astrology, you're likely on all the committees and volunteering to lead the charge when it comes to adopting new technology or software. You are likely to be the one coordinating Friday Night drinks and often have intuitive flashes of genius that leave your coworkers gobsmacked.

The Sixth House in Pisces

If Pisces is on the cusp of your Sixth House, you need to remember to get in steps while at work, and make sure to keep a water bottle on hand to hydrate. Depression can be an issue so it's best to find a job that makes you feel as if you are living up to your potential.

PUTTING IT
ALL TOGETHER

Many planets in Quadrant Two indicate that in this lifetime, your primary attention is focused on yourself—on developing a heightened awareness of your personal identity and inherent values, learning to be more at ease in communicating your ideas to others.

You probably need more time alone than other folks in order to stay in touch with your own identity and experience yourself personally—recognizing your own impulses and learning to discriminate when and how to appropriately assert yourself. Staying grounded is important, as things do not turn out well when you "leave yourself" in order to impress others.

When someone has an opinion different from yours, you are learning to "check it out" inside yourself and take the time to think things through, rather than making an impulsive retort based on wanting to impress. You are learning the value of staying centered inside yourself while relating with others.

This is a lifetime designed for learning more about your personality, how you feel inside yourself, and where you really stand. You are learning to get in touch with what makes you feel comfortable, what you inherently value, and what gives you a true sense of self-worth.

It's also a learning/teaching lifetime, and through interacting with a variety of people you will grow and discover more about yourself.

Do you have a majority of planets in your second quadrant? This is a strong sign that one of your goals in this lifetime is to learn how to balance your sense of self against your relationship to others.

You will benefit from self-care and not neglecting your personal pleasure, and when you find mediums to explore your creativity, doors to thriving and joy will be opened to you.

Be sure to focus on healthy routines for diet and exercise, and to notice where you make choices that allow for a more efficient use of time.

Your personal life will be one of your greatest teachers, as your family, children, friends, and coworkers will provide endless lessons to explore yourself.

DIG DEEPER

Does your work get you excited? Are you upskilling? How is your work contributing (or not) to you building the life you want?

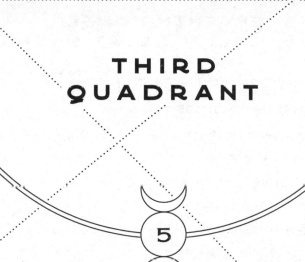

THIRD QUADRANT

5

The Third Quadrant of the Astrology Wheel inhabits the Seventh, Eighth, and Ninth houses. This is the area that speaks to relationships, intimacy, and mind expansion, which means learning to merge with others out in society is key to this quadrant. If you have heaps of planets here you love to relate and attach to others on the regular.

SEVENTH HOUSE
AKA HOUSE OF RELATIONSHIPS

RELATED SIGN AND PLANET: Libra and Venus

AREAS OF INFLUENCE: Relationships, marriage

POSITIVE ATTRIBUTE: Attracting positive and fair people into your life

NEGATIVE ATTRIBUTE: Aligning yourself with lower-vibe folks

HOW TO BALANCE: Finding a healthy way to form relationships and connections

The Seventh House is also sometimes referred to as the House of Marriage, but really, it pulls in just about everyone you deal with. From business partners to romantic liaisons, friends to acquaintances, the Seventh House reveals the sort of people we attract. The cusp of this sector is where the Descendant lies, opposite from our Ascendant—that First House cusp that reveals what it is we put out into the world. So while, yes, you can see what sort of partnerships you attract with the Descendant, it also reveals what you think you *lack*. A-Ha! Now we're getting to the heart of this house. Whatever sign or planets inhabit your Seventh House is where you think you're incomplete. It's total hogwash, of course, but it's how we all feel about it even though we are complete and perfect beings.

Of course, this realm can act like our shadow side too. We project onto others what we really can't stand about ourselves. Interestingly enough, it was heavy Seventh Houser Carl Jung who coined that famous "shadow" term. Carl had both his Sun and Uranus in this sector, revealing his love of understanding others and attracting some unusual types in the process.

People with a strong Seventh House are here to connect and merge. They are highly charismatic types, who excel in one-on-one relationships and love all sorts of healthy rapports. Here are the social butterflies, the artists, the diplomats, and the dictators. They usually have heaps of people swirling around them as they are insanely popular, outshining every last one of us with good, strong, relationship values. Seventh House people can greatly alter other people's lives as they tend to focus a great deal on relationships, so remember to use that for good and not ill (some folks with a strong Seventh House trend toward an interest in foreign affairs). After all, Hitler had a strong Seventh House.

Like Jung, the creator of psychoanalysis, Sigmund Freud, also had his Sun and Uranus in the Seventh House, as well as Mercury, indicating a strong and innovative need to reestablish the balance in others. In truth both he and Jung needed people as much as they helped people. Seventh House people can't really achieve happiness without others. But it's the equality in how they treat people that's the real cause for their bliss.

The Seventh House in Aries

If you have Aries in the cusp of your Seventh House, you are passionate but can also be quick to anger. Obviously, that can do some serious damage so make sure to make mindfulness a part of your daily practice! You also probably want to call most of the shots in a relationship, which means you're likely suited to someone who appreciates your decisive and lively personality.

The Seventh House in Taurus

If you've got Taurus in your Seventh House then you're not the type to enjoy small talk on a first date. Bar banter gives you hives. You want to dive headlong into serious stuff, which might scare off some who feel like you're too intense. You'll thrive with a stable, calming partner who gives you a deep sense of security and is going to be your ride or die no matter what the world throws at you.

The Seventh House in Gemini

If Gemini is in your Seventh House, you're going to need to get involved with people who can stimulate your mind. You're also not going to be one for ultimatums. Relationships will unfold organically in your life or not at all. If people try to force it, you're headed for the door.

The Seventh House in Cancer

Have a Seventh House in the sign of Cancer? You are highly sensitive in relationships and need someone who is careful with your feelings and loves you even when you are shower crying. When you find your person, you are going to be their rock through any difficult moments.

The Seventh House in Leo

If your Seventh House is in Leo, you have good self-awareness and tend to attract people who want to bask in your light. In love, you might actually let your partner handle many of the household decisions so you can focus your powerful energy on other facets of your world.

The Seventh House in Virgo

Have a Seventh House in Virgo? Then you are going to want to find a person who has the skills and personality traits that you, yourself, might be lacking. You have a practical, pragmatic take on relationships and prefer to find one where you each complement the other.

The Seventh House in Libra

When you have a Seventh House in Libra, you might be a little, ahem, picky when choosing a partner. But even though you choose a partner carefully, what is going to make you happiest is a person who is happy to compromise and realizes that long-term relationships are a give-and-take, not a winner-take-all situation. When you finally settle on a special someone, make sure it's a person who loves to compromise—that will make you the most comfortable.

The Seventh House in Scorpio

Scorpio in the Seventh House might have difficult love affairs in their younger years, but with any luck learn from those early mistakes to mature into an adult who has a good handle on their character traits. Loyalty is your love language.

The Seventh House in Sagittarius

If you have a cusp on the Seventh House in Sagittarius then you want to get involved with a social butterfly. You're going to flee from anyone too clingy, and you're all about encouraging your lover to have independent pursuits.

The Seventh House in Capricorn

When your Seventh House is in the sign of Capricorn, you have high standards. While that's fine, make sure that you aren't so picky that you find fault in minor things. You might be the kind of person who settles down later in life than most of your friends.

The Seventh House in Aquarius

If you have Aquarius in your Seventh House then you have a secret fear of losing your powerful sense of self to a relationship. Communication is the key here (although be careful of being too judgmental). You will likely be happiest as part of a couple that has regular check-ins.

The Seventh House in Pisces

When your Seventh House is in Pisces, you want a vibrant, joyful person that loves living a creative life. Your personality can be strong so theirs should be too. You might benefit from a weekly creative night together where you paint, read aloud, write, or watch art house films.

DIG DEEPER

What types of people do you tend to attract in relationships? What qualities do you feel are missing in partners, and what would you like to cultivate? Complete this sentence: "I wish I had someone to share . . ."

EIGHTH HOUSE
AKA HOUSE OF
TRANSFORMATION

RELATED SIGN AND PLANET: Scorpio and Pluto

AREAS OF INFLUENCE: Sex, death and rebirth, other people's money

POSITIVE ATTRIBUTE: Merging yourself deeply on an intimate basis

NEGATIVE ATTRIBUTES: Power struggles and domination

HOW TO BALANCE: Assisting others in their own personal transformations

It's a powerful realm, the Eighth House. Chock-full of mystery and the occult, it's the house that deals with death, destruction, sex, and inheritances. But at its heart, the pulse of this house is POWER. Oh, you'll know a thing or two about it if you have the Sun or Moon or several planets here. You know about control too, or lack thereof. It's a dark and brooding house, where the macabre and spooky lurk. It's the house of Scorpio and Pluto—the God of the Underworld. It plumbs the depths of the soul, and that's exactly what strong Eighth Housers are born to do. They live for secrets, for crisis, and for depth-fueled intimacy.

There's no better soul that can handle a critical situation like a healthy Eighth House. They simply live for it. Calm and collected in the most nerve-wracking of scenarios, strong Eighth House types swoop in and assist the rest of us when we're at our worst. That's why so many healers and therapists have a strong Eighth House. Tycoons too, for they make fabulous money managers. They keep secrets about your psyche, *and* your money.

This is also a very sexual house and can point to our deepest, darkest desires. When we come into deep connections with others, what do we lose to have such communion? How do our needs and cravings change? Evolve? Die or find rebirth?

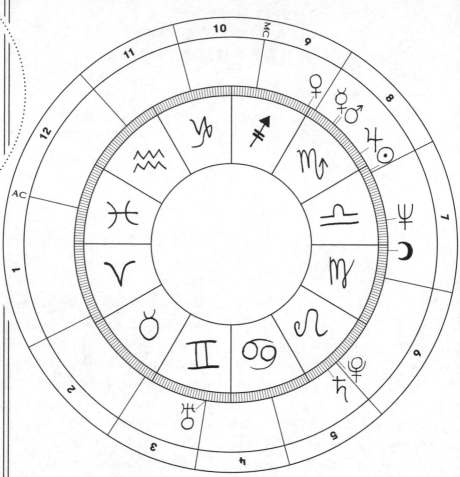

Take a look at mega Eighth Houser Deepak Chopra. Not only does he have the Sun, Jupiter, Neptune, Mars, and Mercury in this realm, he also has Uranus opposite his Midheaven, or career cusp. Indicating a revolutionary and innovative career path. Chopra is a self-described "world-renowned pioneer in integrative medicine and personal transformation." Welp, can't get more Eighth House than that! His very existence is to unleash our potential through mind-body healing. It's only an extra added plus that the ruler of his Eighth House sits in the publishing realm. Deepak has published eighty-nine books on alternative medicine and transformation.

The Eighth House in Aries

If you have an Eighth House in Aries, then you love taboo topics and enjoy dropping them into conversations. Money, politics, sex, religion? Those are awesome conversation topics—you don't get what all the fuss is about. You aren't known for your patience and want things to happen now or, actually, could they happen yesterday? When big things go down in your life you are highly independent and so prefer to deal with them on your own.

The Eighth House in Taurus

When you have an Eighth House in Taurus, you are frugal unless you're spoiling someone special like a significant other. You're not a fast adapter to change, and you'll likely hang back during uncertainty or tumult to assess which way the wind will blow.

The Eighth House in Gemini

If Gemini is on the cusp of your Eighth House you might have a tendency to be too nosy in conversations. The good news is that you don't hide from your problems or shy away from challenges . . . and you'd prefer to be considered as curious, thanks very much. And in the bedroom, you love that dirty talk.

The Eighth House in Cancer

When your Eighth House is in Cancer, you aren't the sort to post private details of your life in Instagram stories. Sometimes people might find you off-putting because you are so private and reserved. You might have a hard time reaching orgasm with someone you aren't deeply connected to on an emotional level.

The Eighth House in Leo

When Leo is in your Eighth House, self-esteem is normally not an issue. The challenge for you is going to be tamping down that big ego to make space for others. You likely make a big production out of sex, and might get noise complaints if you share a bedroom wall with a neighbor.

The Eighth House in Virgo

If you have Virgo in your Eighth House you aren't going to wake up in a strange bed or go on a stress-fueled online shopping binge. Your archetype might be "The Virgin," but that doesn't mean you are a prude. You also know what you want in the bedroom and don't see anything wrong with critiquing a partner's performance. If you push your comfort zones you might find transformation waiting around the corner.

The Eighth House in Libra

When your Eighth House is in Libra, you are the kind of person who acts like a duck—seemingly serene on the surface but frantically paddling underwater. You achieve great success when you can form a true partnership where responsibilities are divided and shared—in fact, you might make lovemaking a chore chart!

The Eighth House in Scorpio

When Scorpio is on the cusp of your Eighth House, you spend a lot of time pondering the deeper questions about the meaning of life. You are also secretive about your money, which can be an issue if you don't want to bring a partner into your financial planning. Sex can be a real power play, and you are often known as the horndog of the zodiac for your relentless appetite.

The Eighth House in Sagittarius

If your Eighth House is in Sagitarrius you might find yourself thinking a lot about death (like if I die tomorrow what have I accomplished?) and sex (what's my kinkiest sexual fantasy?). You are likely to do a lot of research or consult a financial advisor before making money-related decisions.

The Eighth House in Capricorn

When your Eighth House is death, you are focused on your legacy. Why are you here? What are you meant to do? How will you leave your mark? You might be an attentive lover, but when you begin obsessing over finding a gray pubic hair or whether your boobs are getting saggy you begin to lose excitement. Try to take a more lighthearted approach to aging and remember getting older is a privilege denied to many.

The Eighth House in Aquarius
When your Eighth House is in Aquarius you like to live on the wild side when it comes to money and sex. Vegas might be a fun trip for you—as long as you remember not to bet it all on red! Try not to overindulge and remember that balance doesn't have to be boring.

The Eighth House in Pisces
When your Eighth House has Pisces on the cusp, you might need to spend ample time at the nail salon because you likely chew your fingernails to the nubs. A natural worrier, you can practice self-care with yoga and meditation. You also worry about making mistakes with money, but if you can learn that sometimes you win some and sometimes you lose, you might be able to be more relaxed. Sexual fantasies *really* work for you.

DIG DEEPER

The Eighth House is often a place where we connect with death and rebirth. Are you uncomfortable thinking about your own mortality? Why or why not? What would you like said at your funeral? What does a successful aging experience look like to you?

NINTH HOUSE
AKA HOUSE OF PHILOSOPHY

RELATED SIGN AND PLANET: Sagittarius and Jupiter

AREAS OF INFLUENCE: Travel, education, all things mind-expansion

POSITIVE ATTRIBUTES: Cultivating information and teaching the rest of us

NEGATIVE ATTRIBUTE: Becoming too dogmatic with your beliefs

HOW TO BALANCE: Learn to see the big picture

Intellectual growth and mind expansion rule the Ninth House. This is the sector of the Astrology Wheel associated with free-spirited Sagittarius and the far-reaching and optimistic planet Jupiter. The Ninth House reveals our travel tendencies. It denotes where we like to go on an adventure and get a bird's-eye view—psychically *and* intellectually through higher education, philosophy, religion, and ethics. This is the realm of the higher mind, where we discover our quest for understanding. The sign that guides your Ninth House shows us where we crave meaning and seek experiences different from our own.

You're a born teacher if you have a compelling Ninth House. A big mouth too, but at least it's educated! You challenge our intellectual boundaries and never stop learning—and that's fabulous for the rest of us. Lawyers, talk show hosts, college professors, and travel agents often have strong showings in this realm.

The Ninth House is also heavily associated with publishing, broadcasting, and advertising. Knowledge and, just as importantly, sharing that knowledge is everything to them. The Ninth House also divulges how *other* people talk to us. In contrast to our own voice shown by the Third House.

Let's take a look at the chart of actor and talk show host Whoopi Goldberg. Whoopi has her Leo Sun, Venus, Pluto, and Mercury all packed in the Ninth House. She's actually quite a secretive person with

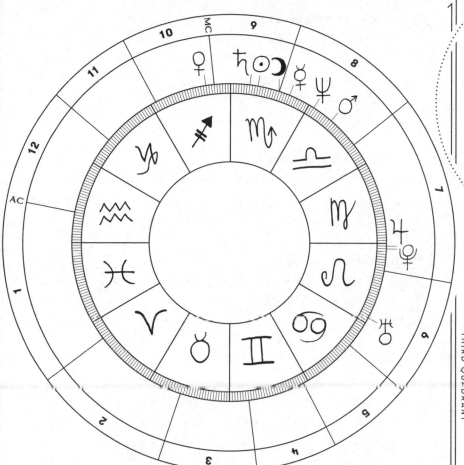

her Scorpio Rising and Moon, but her voice cannot be stopped with the majority of her planets placed high in the broadcasting house! Sure, she says some rather shocking and abrupt things with her Mercury in a hard angle with the planet of shock and surprise, Uranus. But to us, she's pure genius.

The Ninth House in Aries

If your Ninth House is in Aries you often believe that you are drawing power from another source, be it a traditional religion or a more vaguely defined spirit (maybe even your own deep sense of self). You might also love to learn about world religions even if you don't practice them.

The Ninth House in Taurus

In sharp contrast to Aries, when your Ninth House is in Taurus, you are likely not a religious zealot. This position generally takes a pretty darn practical view on religion—namely, don't yuck someone else's yum. You are often going to be focused on what's in front of you rather than navel-gazing on esoteric matters.

The Ninth House in Gemini

When your Ninth House is in Gemini, then your belief system is founded in logic and reason. You might also enjoy dabbling in different spiritual or philosophical practices until you find one that feels right.

The Ninth House in Cancer

When your Ninth House is in Cancer then you might feel called to honor the divine feminine. You also find great spiritual nourishment by traveling to lovely places that restore your soul.

The Ninth House in Leo

If your Ninth House is in Leo then you are going to find solace during difficult times by pulling up your roots and heading out on the open road for a new place to plant them. You might jump around religious or spiritual practices. You also have a sunny outlook on humanity.

The Ninth House in Virgo

When your Ninth House is in Virgo, your skepticism makes it hard to believe in things that lack scientific evidence. Rather than mock religion or spirituality, you would be wise to approach it from a place of honest curiosity. Who knows, you might learn something!

The Ninth House in Libra

When you have Libra on the cusp of your Ninth House, your church might well be the natural environment and your religion could be acts of service to others. You are going to derive soul-deep satisfaction working for justice.

The Ninth House in Scorpio

If Scorpio is in your Ninth House, you might be attracted to the occult or mysticism. To you, the pursuit of knowledge is what's important, even if it sends you down rabbit holes that others might find uncomfortable.

The Ninth House in Sagittarius

When your Ninth House is in Sagittarius, you love to visit new places and nothing fills your bucket quite like setting out for new horizons. You need travel, to learn and experience new things on a regular basis. You're optimistic and can indulge in the finer things. Your glass isn't just half full, it's overflowing with champagne! Just remember to take a reality check now and again.

The Ninth House in Capricorn

If you have Capricorn in your Ninth House you might be attracted to religious leaders or spiritual gurus. With that being said, you still have a great appreciation for data and facts. Please don't push your convictions on everyone around you. When it comes to travel, you'd prefer to visit a familiar destination where you know you'll have a good time. Practicality and comfort are the keys here.

The Ninth House in Aquarius

If Aquarius is in your Ninth House then you might have a traditional world outlook. As a result, traveling is a must, even if it's just to another part of your neighborhood—it's essential for you to interact with folks who make you question your belief systems.

The Ninth House in Pisces

With Pisces in that Ninth House you are curious about what lies beyond the unseen veil. Consulting psychics, practicing tarot, or studying astrology (hello!) makes you feel fulfilled. You also are attracted to practices that spread peace and love to humanity as a whole. You are going to be happiest taking a trip to a lake or booking a beach house.

PUTTING IT
ALL TOGETHER

Do you see a majority of your planets in this Third Quadrant? If so, you are on a life's mission to become more aware of others, rather than being so self-focused. You want "another half" but to succeed you need to be willing to allow others around you to grow. As you open to meet their influence and energetic contributions, your transformation will give them energy too.

Lots of planets here also reveal that you are destined for partnership in this lifetime, so there will never be a lack of candidates. If your commitment to your partner is strong enough, you will be open to learning from them, which will help you express your authentic identity, which will then allow you to develop and refine the expression of your own identity.

As this transformation sets in, you will actually gain more than you may have imagined going into the relationship.

DIG DEEPER

What types of travel nourish your spirit? Are you religious, or do you view yourself as spiritual? How does that impact your life? If you aren't active in those areas, do you want to be? Why or why not?

FOURTH QUADRANT

6

The Fourth Quadrant of the Astrology Wheel contains the Tenth, Eleventh, and Twelfth houses. Unlike the First Quadrant, which begins with the self, the last quadrant is all about *everyone else.*

This is the realm that tells us about our worldly ambitions, career, community, and service to humanity. How you naturally align yourself with humankind and how you fit into the world is the foundation of the quadrant.

TENTH HOUSE
AKA HOUSE OF STATUS

RELATED SIGN AND PLANET: Capricorn and Saturn

AREAS OF INFLUENCE: Career, vocation, public reputation

POSITIVE ATTRIBUTES: Achievement and success

NEGATIVE ATTRIBUTE: Irresponsibility with your power

HOW TO BALANCE: Finding your leadership skills within

The high-profile Tenth House reveals how we take our place in the world. It shows our career, our social status, and our ambitions. It's also where that Midheaven or MC is located—that point at the very top of our chart that represents our aspirations and achievements. The Tenth House also has a lot to do with authority figures, our bosses, and our parents (mostly our mother).

The House of Status is a very visible place. If you have quite a few planets here or are having a big surge of planets transiting through this area, you are unlikely to have much privacy. Strong Tenth Housers live their life in a goldfish bowl so to speak—there is no sneaking off to hide, and it seems like almost everything they do is splashed across social media, or the pages of *Us Weekly*. Many celebrities inhabit a heavy Tenth House. People just seem fascinated by them.

This is the realm of moguls, executives, politicians, the famous, and the infamous. People with heaps of planets here can't avoid the spotlight. You're here to shine in a BIG way, and the world will hold you accountable for every single thing that you do. That's why it's extra imperative that your actions are always honorable and reputable. Shady negotiations, secretive love affairs, or any covert operations will be visible. The world expects a lot from big Tenth Housers, so you'd better deliver!

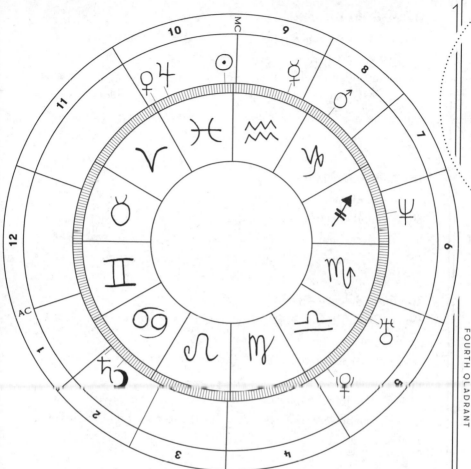

Take a peek at the chart of actress Drew Barrymore. Drew has her Pisces Sun, Jupiter, and Venus all in the ambitious and worldly Tenth House. Sure, she was born to be a film star on name alone, but I don't think I know a single soul who *doesn't* know of her troubled past or have at least some inkling of where she is on her journey these days. Girl is VISIBLE. It's basically her cosmic destiny to be a powerful somebody! Drew's Midheaven is in Aquarius, which means her Tenth House ruler is Uranus, located in the very theatrical and dramatic Fifth House. Her acting claim to fame.

The Tenth House in Aries

When your Tenth House is in Aries, you might have been the product of a difficult pregnancy that's left lingering birth trauma. If that is the case, this trauma might manifest in personal insecurity, anxiety, or a tendency for guilt. You might find deep healing in indulging in childlike joys and journaling. The journey to healing your inner child is lifelong but as you get braver, doors will open. A daily mantra for you is "I am worthy."

The Tenth House in Taurus

If your Tenth House is in Taurus, you are "of the body." You are very physical and benefit from a regular exercise program (and, yes, working up a sweat between the sheets totally counts). You are going to need to love and connect deeply to your work to be motivated to succeed.

The Tenth House in Gemini

When Gemini is in that Tenth House, it's safe to say that you are a social butterfly. You might also have a bad habit of gossip. You will be your best self if you work to drop your guard and embrace your beautiful authentic self. Do this, and you'll raise everyone around you as well. You'll be happiest in roles that are intellectually stimulating, and you might work two jobs that are rather different. This might seem exhausting to others but fulfilling to you.

The Tenth House in Cancer

If Cancer is in that Tenth House then your family of origin might have an outsized impact on the way you show up in the world. Working for a family business is quite possible, or you could have a future as a PTA president if you have kids. You might even choose to be a stay-at-home parent. Just make sure to keep hold of your own sense of self.

The Tenth House in Leo

If your Tenth House is in Leo, you likely are a person who manages people. Make sure that you back up that desire by acquiring some new abilities so that in addition to having all the confidence to be the boss, you have the management skills as well.

The Tenth House in Virgo

When your Tenth House is in Virgo, you might struggle with getting in your own way. Remember that you can achieve what you set your mind to so don't be afraid to aim high. You might dislike being in roles where you have to do a lot of public speaking. Working as an author, blogger, journalist, or anything else that relies on the written word will likely bring satisfaction (as long as you don't judge yourself too harshly).

The Tenth House in Libra

When your Tenth House is in Libra, you might be tempted to give up your power to others. Finding your soulmate is a huge motivator and you might put priority to that higher than other areas. You'll also work well in partnerships as long as the workloads are divvied up fairly.

The Tenth House in Scorpio

When your Tenth House is in Scorpio, you don't have time to skim through life's shallows. You want to be free dive into the darkness and see what hides below. You might have an unusual career for society, like a mortician, erotic writer, or cyber security professional. You are attracted to callings that deal in taboos or secrets. What's off-putting to some is usually fascinating to you.

The Tenth House in Sagittarius

If your Tenth House is in Sagittarius then you might enjoy working in a foreign country or with immigrants. You also might cycle through careers, jumping from one profession to another while searching for what fulfills you.

The Tenth House in Capricorn

Got a Tenth House that begins in Capricorn? Then you aren't going to be a person who is afraid to go for what they want. You may have a karmic debt to repay and as a result need to take on a great deal of responsibility and causes that sometimes might feel a little thankless. But it will be worth it—the success you earn might come later in life.

The Tenth House in Aquarius

When Aquarius is in your Tenth House, you march to the beat of your own drum. You love avant-garde things, but also have an affinity for long-range planning. You tend to think in terms of what's beyond the horizon, and futures others haven't yet imagined.

The Tenth House in Pisces

If your Tenth House is in Pisces, you might not have a clear sense of your path, and do a bit of waffling along the way, but that's okay! You are likely going to find the most joy on a soul-deep level either with the arts or by caring for others, possibly by working in the medical field. Don't like people that much? No worries, you'll also make an excellent vet or vet tech.

DIG DEEPER

What is your ideal definition of success? What is the single most significant change I can make this year to put me on the path for achieving that success? What might I need to let go of that's not serving me toward this goal?

ELEVENTH HOUSE
AKA HOUSE OF FRIENDSHIPS

RELATED SIGN AND PLANET: Aquarius and Uranus

AREAS OF INFLUENCE: Friends, community, hopes and wishes

POSITIVE ATTRIBUTE: Thriving at being a team player

NEGATIVE ATTRIBUTE: Becoming too much of a follower

HOW TO BALANCE: Learning how to lead a group while being an individual

The Eleventh House rules your social scene, group dynamics, your idea of utopia, and teamwork. It's an unconventional house, linked with the sign of Aquarius and the wild and eclectic planet Uranus. This is the sector where you dream big and want to change the world. But that's hard to do all by your lonesome! That's why this is also the house that exposes what you're like in a group. You've got to find like-minded individuals who are on your wavelength to make an impact, and those dynamics are what the Eleventh House is all about!

This realm shows what kinds of friends you gravitate toward. Do you like a lot or a few? Best friends only or lots of acquaintances? This is where your associations lie, your networking skills, and any groups you decide to join. And join you must if you have a strong Eleventh House! After all, good Eleventh Housers are here to make an impression on the world. They're activists who fight for a cause and they need all the help they can get. They make great leaders, as long as they understand *they are part of a group*. Like a cog in the wheel, but they also must stay true individuals. Remaining true to yourself while you integrate with others is key to this domain.

Your kindred spirits inhabit this house, and so do your hopes and wishes. For this reason, any future planning or long-distance goals are also reflected in this realm. That's why it's so imperative that those with a heavy Eleventh House dream often and dream big. In fact, the bigger, the better! These folks can change the world if they really want to! Check out the chart of actress and activist Jane Fonda.

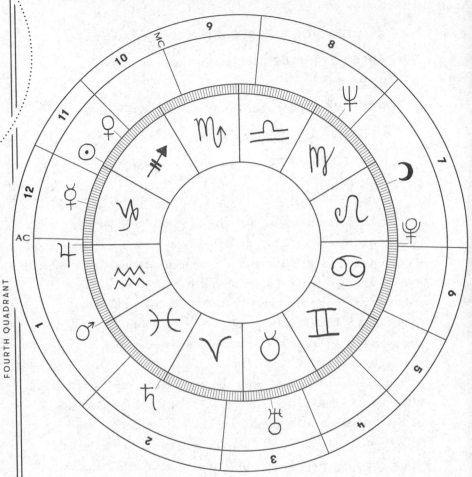

Jane is very Eleventh House with her Sagittarius Sun and Venus here. She has no problem standing up for what's right and fighting for her cause of the moment. And by the way, simply being a Sag means her crusade du jour can change on a whim. See Jane's Moon in Leo opposite feisty and aggressive Mars? She challenges people and isn't afraid of a fight. In fact, back in December of 2019, she was arrested for the fifth time in her life while protesting climate change. She's a true activist through and through and all at the tender age of eighty-two! Never stop dreaming, all you Eleventh Housers. You guys can really do some powerful things.

The Eleventh House in Aries

If your Eleventh House begins in Aries, you make friends easily but don't always keep them. You might at times be overcompetitive and that can create conflict in your social circles. Remember to give as well as take from others.

The Eleventh House in Taurus

When your Eleventh House is in Taurus you take care of the people you love and meet them where they are in this life. If you work to cultivate emotional stability, you can look forward to a joyful and secure old age where you reap the benefits of a life well lived.

The Eleventh House in Gemini

If that Eleventh House is in Gemini, you likely enjoy being on the phone, chatting, texting, and staying in touch. But you may struggle to have deep relationships as a result. You might thrive by creating online groups where you can chat away while building more meaningful connections.

The Eleventh House in Cancer

When your Eleventh House begins in Cancer, you love hanging with family and generally consider them your best friends. One challenge for you is to practice positive self-talk. Look for ways to make this a part of your daily life.

The Eleventh House in Leo

If you've got Leo roaring in your Eleventh House, you might put a lot of importance on *who* you are friends with and, more to the point, how good they make you look. Your journey in this life is to put less focus on image and status and more on surrounding yourself with decent and kind people. It will do your heart and personal happiness a lot of good!

The Eleventh House in Virgo

Have Virgo in your Eleventh House? You might have had friends who didn't serve you well. There could even be some deep betrayals here.

However, if you have the courage to keep your heart open, you'll likely be able to attract quality people into your orbit.

The Eleventh House in Libra

If your Eleventh House is in Libra, it comes as no surprise that you want balance in your friendships. Remember that nobody is ever going to be perfect, so work to love those in your life for the perfectly imperfect beings they are (just like you).

The Eleventh House in Scorpio

If you have your Eleventh House in Scorpio, you are a friend for life. A true "ride or die," you are going to be alongside your friends no matter what (for better, and sadly, for worse). You likely have a biting wit and might have issues with your family of origin. Problems can arise if you don't deal with family issues and emotional blockages.

The Eleventh House in Sagittarius

When your Eleventh House is in the sign of Sagittarius, you are usually the hub of an eclectic and dynamic social circle. You might have friends who are wildly different from each other in worldview, hobbies, and habits, but you know variety is the spice of life.

The Eleventh House in Capricorn

If you've got a Capricorn in your Eleventh House then friendships are serious business. You might hunker down with a clique of associates from work and call it good. You are also a consummate networker because friendships that benefit you are useful and practical.

The Eleventh House in Aquarius

If you've got Aquarius on the cusp of your Eleventh House then you might prefer strong friendships with those who value working toward a higher purpose, just like you. You might make good friends in activist circles or volunteer groups.

The Eleventh House in Pisces

If you have your Pisces in your Eleventh House, you might have a tendency to attract people into your life who take more than they give. On the bright side, you don't need to see your friends every day to keep a deep connection. You might well be one of those people who don't see a friend for years, and then pick right back up where they left off.

DIG DEEPER

Think back to your childhood friendships. How are they different—and similar—to your adult friendships now? What kind of support do you wish you had more of? How are you learning to be a better friend?

TWELFTH HOUSE
AKA HOUSE OF
SERVICE & SPIRITUALITY

RELATED SIGN AND PLANET: Pisces and Neptune

AREAS OF INFLUENCE: Psychic abilities, dreams, secrets, emotions, karma

POSITIVE ATTRIBUTE: Using your powers to emotionally rehabilitate others

NEGATIVE ATTRIBUTES: Inner suffering and secret affairs

HOW TO BALANCE: Learning to be of service to others is the way to help yourself

The Twelfth House is probably one of the most misunderstood houses in the Astrology Wheel. It's often been called the House of Undoing, and heaps of old astrology books have been written around horrible Twelfth House challenges like prison, confinement, illnesses, and hospitalization. Fun stuff, eh? But it's not so! The Twelfth House is a magical place where things not yet seen reside. In fact, people with a strong Twelfth House are generally quite artistic, intuitive, and very, very psychic.

This is the realm of the unseen. Perhaps that's why it was so heavily linked with confinement. Or maybe because the types of people who inhabit the very spiritual Twelfth House are so mystical and strange themselves. They're healers too. The evolved ones instinctively know what we need and they have a brilliant, empathic ability to connect. The less evolved are escapists who feel like no one understands them so they plot secret affairs and knock back bottles of whiskey. Give 'em time. The old phrase "Serve or Suffer" was coined for this very house. It's true too, self-sacrifice is a big part of this realm.

This is also the house where we rest and retreat. In fact, if you've got quite a lot of planets transiting your Twelfth House you'll feel safer and more comfortable being alone in your own private sanctuary— wherever that may be. Probably doing some meditation, yoga, tarot cards, tea leaves, or some other sort of deep soul-searching. People who have heavy Twelfth Houses often feel like their true selves are not entirely seen. Some have a hard time knowing who they are. But all believe that something very powerful lies just on the other side of the veil. They feel it, and they know it.

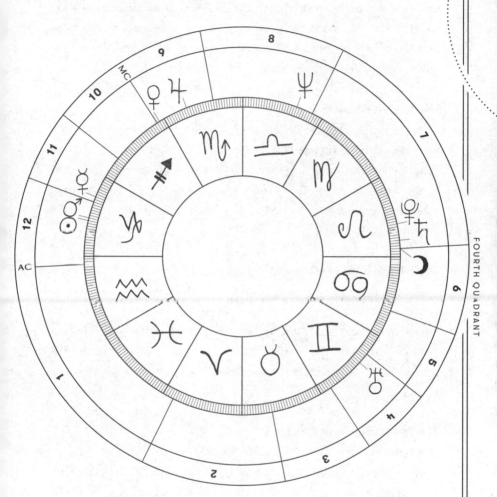

Take a look at the chart of musician David Bowie. David was born with his Capricorn Sun, Mars, and Mercury all in the Twelfth House and all squared by mystical and inspirational Neptune. He was a musical gift to us. An artist, a genius, and a rebel thanks to his Aquarius Rising. Bowie helped untold amounts of people through his music and his androgynous looks. He gave a voice to the voiceless. A true Twelfth House.

The Twelfth House in Aries

People who have Aries at the cusp of their Twelfth House might have had former lives that were cut short or ended in violence. This might leave you protective of yourself and easily wounded. While you might present a face to the world that seems confident and resilient, inwardly you might feel barbs easily. If you are lucky to get to a place where you are comfortable in your own skin, then you can take charge of the situation and not leave yourself vulnerable to others.

The Twelfth House in Taurus

When your Twelfth House astrology is on the cusp of Taurus, you might show the world one face, and hide your deeper, private self. You could well be the life of the party, and then go home stressed over your credit card balance or inbox. You are better off limiting friendships to those perceptive folks who really value you for the loyal, trustworthy person you are.

The Twelfth House in Gemini

If you see Gemini on the cusp of your Twelfth House you probably do your best creative work alone; however, you still crave recognition from others. You might struggle with feelings of self-worth and feel jealous of those with perfectly curated Instagram feeds. Your task in this life is to focus less on other people and more on your own creative work to know true joy.

The Twelfth House in Cancer

Do you spy Cancer in your Twelfth House? If so, you don't like to wear your feelings on your sleeve. You also might be part of a family with some skeletons in their closet or harbor complicated feelings about one, or both, of your parents. You have a hard time coming out of your shell, but that's the only way you can really connect.

The Twelfth House in Leo

Folks whose Twelfth House is in Leo have a big ol' personality, but they know how to keep it under wraps. While you have big dreams you often are like a tender sapling that likes to grow in another's shadow. These ambitions might be tied to having had a very successful past life. You are going to feel most fulfilled in service to others. You just gotta be useful!

The Twelfth House in Virgo
Do you have Virgo in your Twelfth House? If so, are you the kind of person who is always running to the doctor convinced that you have a mysterious disease. Careful, because worrying too much is bad for your health! You're also likely to hide (and thereby surprise others) just how awesomely useful you really are.

The Twelfth House in Libra
When your Twelfth House is in Libra you crave a soul-deep connection with a partner, but you might also attract people who damage your trust. Once you learn to make your expectations more realistic, and you try to find the patience to deal with other people (humans, ugh), then you can start to thrive.

The Twelfth House in Scorpio
If you have Scorpio in your Twelfth House, I'm not saying you have a secret BDSM dungeon, but I'm not *not* saying that either. In reality, you likely do have a pull to some dark urges, but there is conflict there. Unleash what you keep hidden from the world and become a force of reckoning.

The Twelfth House in Sagittarius
Have Sagittarius in your Twelfth House? You are great at seeing the better side of humanity. You might be inclined to hide some of that sunny optimism and playful nature, but I wish you wouldn't because it's oh so fun to be around you.

The Twelfth House in Capricorn
Okay, you Capricorn Twelfth House folks, we know you want to front like you're some big rebel. You might pretend to be super edge. But, se-

cretly, you know that what you really want is to be home in your comfy pajamas, out of the spotlight, and preferably with a good book.

The presence of benefic planets in one's natal chart will ensure the feelings of security and wisdom.

The Twelfth House in Aquarius

When Aquarius is in your Twelfth House, you don't want to be the kind of person who stands out, even if you might have been born to do so. You might seek relationships but what you really crave is freedom. This is your ultimate goal in this life. As a result, spirituality or some sort of "connecting to source" might help you channel that frustration into a positive outlet.

The Twelfth House in Pisces

When you have a Twelfth House in Pisces, you might show up in spaces as a snarky and antagonistic force, while once folks get to know you they discover a lovable marshmallow. You are afraid to be vulnerable, and so guard that sweet side. It's a shame, but those who get to really know you value it so much.

DIG DEEPER

Do you feel like you are an intuitive person? Why or why not? Do your dreams tell you things? Have you ever had any psychic experiences?

PLANETARY
PATTERNS

7

P hew! We've made it all the way around the Astrology Wheel. We've looked at each house and given you a chance to do some self-reflection. Are you feeling a little steadier on your feet? Does that Astrology Wheel feel more like a friend? Have you already had some insights into what makes you tick? Trust me, astrology is addictive. The more you know, the more you want to know. And we've only just scratched the surface.

Now remember back when we first started looking at the houses? I mentioned that you may have noticed that your natal chart seems to be clumped together in some places and spread out or empty in others. All those lines zigzagging back and forth seem to form some sort of pattern, and guess what? Understanding this component of your chart also provides insight into your identity.

As I've discussed, natal charts come in many different shapes and sizes. Astrologers have identified seven main shapes, but some people don't really have any particular shape at all. No need to fret if you don't fit into any of the below descriptions. It just means your chart is as unique and wildly different as you are!

> **HOT TIP!** Make sure you only use the planets when determining if your natal chart has a core pattern. Extra asteroids, comets, exoplanets (planets that orbit around stars beyond our solar system), and nodes only clutter and confuse the pattern!

The seven different shapes are:

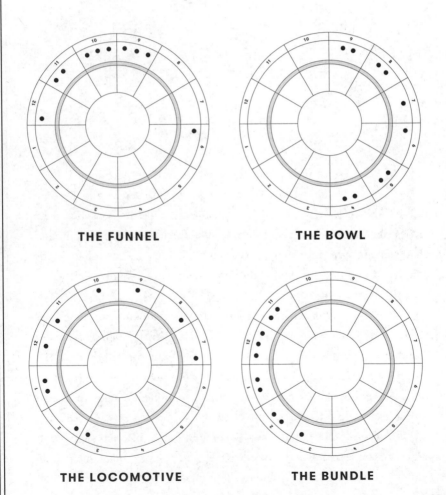

THE FUNNEL

THE BOWL

THE LOCOMOTIVE

THE BUNDLE

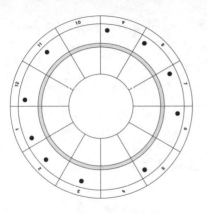

THE SPLASH

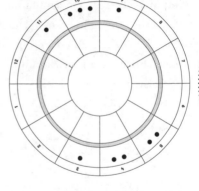

THE SEESAW

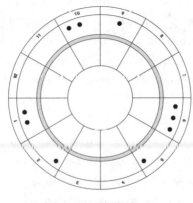

THE SPLAY

THE FUNNEL

The Funnel, or Bucket Chart, is easy to spot. It occurs when half of the chart is filled with planets with the exception of one. This one planet, or singleton, is opposite from all the others, forming a handle on what looks like a bucket shape. Or, you can look at it like all the planets are funneling through that lone planet . . . hence a Funnel Chart. Either way you view it, that singleton planet becomes pretty darn important if you have this chart shape.

People with Funnel Charts are quite goal-oriented. Fixated even. The lone planet depicting a funnel or handle acts as a cosmic focal point that aids in determination and ambition. It's energized and none of the other planets can truly function without going through that single planet first. Of course, the planet, sign, and house of your particular singleton offer incredible insight. Pay attention to it. It's your biggest asset!

THE BOWL

The Bowl Chart looks like, you guessed it, a bowl! If you have this shape in your chart, you'll notice that half of the chart is occupied by planets, while the other half is empty. This chart is very one-sided, which means that people with this chart pattern can be one-sided too. You're also resourceful, independent, and terribly driven. You can be stubborn too, albeit with a great set of values. It feels as if something is always missing in your life, so it becomes your personal mission to find out exactly what that is.

Hint: It's usually other people!

Of course, where the planets fall in your own chart determines where you are feeling that void. If the bowl pattern is above the horizon line in your chart, you will feel as if you're missing out on a more introspective life. If most of the planets are below the horizon line, you're lacking public recognition. Is the bowl pattern to the left? You're feeling a void in the relationship realm, while a heavy right-handed chart might need a little more personal time.

THE LOCOMOTIVE

Like a train running counterclockwise around the Astrology Wheel, the locomotive pattern occurs when two thirds of a chart is taken up by planets, and a third of the chart is empty. You'll feel as if you've got a steam engine running around you if you have this pattern. These folks are driven, compelling, and highly energetic. They have amazing drive and self-discipline and are highly individualistic to boot.

The first planet on the locomotive train is crucial. It's the leader, and you'll learn about yourself and the essence of your chart when you pay extra attention to that lead planet. Find it by first spotting the empty third of the chart wheel and then move counterclockwise. The first planet you come to is the lead! It's the planet of action and initiation, and reveals where and how you should apply talent and initiative.

THE BUNDLE

You've got a Bundle Chart when all of the planets are packed into a third of the chart wheel or less (like sardines in a can). When the majority of your chart is highly concentrated on a specific area, you are just as likely to be condensed. This is the pattern where the specialists lurk, as these types have a natural ability to focus for long stretches of time on a particular subject or interest. Perhaps that's why it's the rarest pattern in the bunch. We can't have everyone acting like an expert, now can we?

These tenacious folks are insanely focused and determined. The downside of this pattern is the sometimes lack of perception and insight with the rest of their chart, which at times simply translates into less empathy or understanding. Bundle types live in their own world. They are immune to outside critique and disapproval.

THE SPLASH

A Splash Chart occurs when all of the planets are strewn around the Astrology Wheel in an even distribution, indicating a versatile and flexible individual. These are the Jacks & Jills of all trades. They excel in many different areas and love to be around diverse groups of people. The splash pattern chart is scattered and at times distracted. Unlike the Bundle, they have a hard time focusing on one thing for too long. Though boredom is seldom an issue with this chart.

Here are the open-minded folks, who bring wide-eyed perspectives and an engaging vibe. You'll often find yourself in a flurry of activity if you have this chart pattern. The downside of the Splash Chart is that people with this pattern tend to spread themselves too thin. Forgoing the time and patience it takes to master a skill can lead to disorganized ambition at some point or another. Learning to slow down and focus is key for this chart.

THE SEESAW

The Seesaw Chart wheel looks just like it sounds, with half of the planets on one side of the chart, and the rest in direct opposition with the others. Balance is the name of the game if you have this pattern. Oh sure, you're probably competitive to boot. This is the chart of athletes, lawyers, and anyone who loves a good ol' fashioned debate. You love to bounce ideas off others and thrive in a healthy form of competition. You need people and you learn through experience.

Those who inhabit a seesaw pattern are epic at seeing every side of a situation. They weigh their options, always with lots of facts and information as their listening skills are usually quite good. The downside is with this placement they can question EVERYTHING. And these types dislike being alone. They always need to bounce ideas off a partner.

THE SPLAY

The Splay Chart is perhaps the most common of the group. It occurs when there are three clusters, or conjunctions, of planets in a chart. Usually in a Splay Chart you'll find at least one trine (that's a special pattern that forms when three planets on a chart are the same distance from each other, creating a triangle; finding this in a chart is believed to speak to confidence, creativity, and deep flow), which means those who are lucky enough to possess this pattern are grounded, fortunate, and confident. If you have a splayed chart, you don't sway to others' demands, and very often ignore the negativity of others. Why bring your own lucky vibe down?

Here lies the self-sufficient individual. Not a fan of any strict routine or binding structures, these folks tend to go their own way while feeling confident in their own decisions and mindset. Of course, the locations where the clusters occur, by sign and by house, paint a clearer picture. But overall, the splay is considered a wonderful pattern to have!

THE LAYOUT

Regardless of whether your chart fits into any of the standard seven patterns or not, you might just learn a lot about yourself or your friends by finding where the majority of the planets reside. Take out your chart and cover up everything below the horizon. Do you have five or more planets up top? Then you are here to be in the spotlight! You love high visibility and you crave being an active part of the world. You are keenly aware of how things work in the worldly sense, and you live to be a part of it. It's basically your job to be part of society. You are outwardly directed and base your responses, reactions, and goals on what is expected from society, business, etc.

If the majority of your planets reside in the lower part or below the horizon line, then you are the subjective type. It's not that you don't have a public life, but you don't need the reassurance from society like top-heavy charters do. People with this orientation are the private types. They are the recluses who tend to gather their strength in private and don't need acceptance from society, which means these folks can actually have a huge impact on the world when they want to. Perhaps it's the fact that they really don't compare themselves to everyone else that is the secret to their success.

Five or more planets on the left side of your Astrology Wheel indicates a go-getter. These are the self-reliant types who prosper on their own initiative and almost never rely on others to make it in this world. Sure, they might need to lean on people every once in a while, but it's basically their mission to be major-league self-starters.

Is the right side of your Astrology Wheel the heaviest? Then you need people. It's almost impossible for you to have success by the sheer force of yourself alone. You are dependent, and lucky for you, you are a natural networker who attracts the right sorts of people to help you get there. No need to rely on your own willpower or self-assertion. You just seem to always be in the right place at the right time.

EMPTY HOUSES

People can freak when they see empty houses in their chart. No planets in my marriage house? Does this mean I'm doomed not to get married? Gah! Nope. Not at all. In fact, there really isn't such a thing as an empty house! At the start of every house cusp you have a sign on that particular house. (Remember, the cusp is the imaginary line that separates a pair of consecutive signs in the zodiac or houses in the horoscope.)

Let's say, for example, that you don't have any planets in your Fifth House (children, art, and romance), but you spy the sign of Virgo on that Fifth House cusp.

An empty house is nothing to fear and is incredibly common. It doesn't mean there isn't any action there, just simply that it's not an area in your life where the main focus is. There isn't a struggle there and that, my dear, can be a very good thing.

EMPTY FIRST HOUSE: A lack of difficulty in your outward persona means less of a struggle with putting yourself out there. The Ascendant AND ruler of Ascendant (planet that is associated with that sign) will reveal any extra strengths and weaknesses.

EMPTY SECOND HOUSE: You are blessed with ease with finances and income and a lack of extra stress around security and stability and earning income. Of course, money issues ebb and flow, but overall this is not your main concern.

EMPTY THIRD HOUSE: Clear communication and conversation and ease of expression make getting your point across less cumbersome. Look to where your Mercury is for extra clues around how you think and speak.

EMPTY FOURTH HOUSE: You lack the burden of any heavy family issues. Well, mostly. We all got 'em! But you probably have it far easier than the rest of us when it comes to dealing with home and family matters.

EMPTY FIFTH HOUSE: Expressions of your love and creative energies flow freely and effortlessly. Look to the ruler of the Fifth House for clues and evidence of all things children, art, and romance.

EMPTY SIXTH HOUSE: Scheduling, organization, and health matters are not massive issues in this lifetime. The Sixth House rules daily work and obligations. Those with an empty house flow with this far easier than the rest of us.

EMPTY SEVENTH HOUSE: Nothing in the House of Relationships? No need to fret! This doesn't mean you're doomed to be single. Far from it! Relating to others is not your main issue in this lifetime. Hard lessons around love are inevitable, but it's less distracting to those with an empty Seventh House.

EMPTY EIGHTH HOUSE: The Eighth House is basically the realm of shared energy. Zero planets here indicate a general comfort around deeper issues and emotional intimacy.

EMPTY NINTH HOUSE: Comfort with seeing the big picture and mind expansion in all forms. Those who don't have any planets in this particular sector may feel less of a need to press their religious and philosophical views on others in this lifetime.

EMPTY TENTH HOUSE: This is where the Midheaven lies, so that will play a heavy factor in determining more about career and reputation based on ruler, by sign, and by house. But generally speaking those with an empty Tenth House find ease in maintaining responsibilities and goals in terms of career and success.

EMPTY ELEVENTH HOUSE: Comfort and ease dealing with groups of people, community, and friendships. Of course, this also rules your hopes and wishes, so check the planet that is your Eleventh House ruler to gain added insight.

EMPTY TWELFTH HOUSE: You might find the world of all things hidden a much more uncomplicated area in your life than others do. Access to your unconscious, dreams, psychic abilities, and the mystical seems to flow more freely to you.

DIG DEEPER

Even though there aren't any celestial bodies residing in an empty house, you can still learn a lot about yourself by checking to see who is the ruler of your Fifth House. In this example, Virgo is associated with the planet Mercury. This means that Mercury is the ruler of your Fifth House! Locating the planetary ruler of this otherwise empty house will now disclose loads of information about your love life and any children you might have.

LET'S TAKE A QUICK PAUSE . . .

Okay, you just took in a lot of information. How are ya'll feeling? Excited? Overwhelmed? Tired? Nervous? Ready to get going? Maybe a combination of all the above.

These feelings are all perfectly normal, especially when learning a whole lot of new information.

Make sure you make a cup of tea or get a glass of water. Stand up. Stretch. This is a marathon, not a sprint.

Once you're back, let's take a moment to reflect on a question from each house.

HOUSE ONE: Do you feel truly seen by those in your life? Why or why not?

HOUSE TWO: Do you feel empowered to gain and attract what resources you need in life? Why or why not?

HOUSE THREE: What types of self-talk do you use? Is it positive or negative? Why?

HOUSE FOUR: How are you making your home a nurturing place?

HOUSE FIVE: What is an activity that brings you deep pleasure? Do you allow yourself to do this enough? Why?

HOUSE SIX: What is one thing you can do today to improve your health or nutrition?

HOUSE SEVEN: Is it easy for you to receive love? Why or why not?

HOUSE EIGHT: Are you satisfied sexually? If not, what do you want to add to that part of your life?

HOUSE NINE: Where do you feel called to travel? Why?

HOUSE TEN: Do you feel you can articulate your life's purpose? If yes, repeat it to yourself. If not, can you make space to reflect on this?

HOUSE ELEVEN: What does community look like for you? How do you show up for that community?

HOUSE TWELVE: How do you define peace for yourself? How do you make space in your life to have it?

Remember, as much as your stars have answers, they also whisper these sorts of questions to you. The universe is never still, and neither are you. You might notice some aspects of yourself at different points in your life, but the important thing is to carve out the time to observe and reflect. Also, this practice will allow you to hone your intuition so you can be better positioned to realize your destiny.

Part **2**

INTERPRETING

YOUR

CHART

YOUR ASCENDANT
& YOUR STYLE

8

N ow that we have gone around the Astrology Wheel and looked at the broader pattern of your chart, you're hopefully getting a good handle on what the stars have to teach you. But if you're like most people, you still have questions about love, career, money, and life. In this section, we're going to delve into some key aspects of life and see how you can use your chart to gain more insight into everyday areas.

As before, we'll take a look at the signs associated with certain houses and now also consider the influence of planets. We'll also examine the charts of some well-known people in light of these questions so you can see how these forces come together and begin to interpret your own chart.

Let's start with the topic that's probably front and center in your mind: Yourself!

We all know that our bone structure, the color of our hair and our eyes are all determined by our DNA. Yes, it is true you are more likely to have Uncle Larry's nose than to share features with those who have similar astrological charts, but for those who pay close attention there are subtle signs that those with the same Ascendant *look* a little bit alike, maybe even have some of the same mannerisms. It is true: Your First House cusp does play a big part in your style, your clothes, your mannerisms, even your body type. So even if you are, say, a go-go-go impatient and fiery Aries, but your Rising Sign is Cancer, you'll end up appearing way more delicate, vulnerable, and dewy than you would otherwise. You won't march right up to people and tell them what you think. You won't wear a bright red bikini either. It's simply not part of that Cancer Ascendant!

Now, if you're surrounded by people you love, you may reveal your true Sun sign nature, but often it's a blessing to take after your Ascendant. Healthy, even! Aligning with your Rising Sign assists you in creating better first impressions. This is even easier if your Venus sign is also in sync with your Ascendant since how you present yourself and what you think is beautiful will align. If it's not, you may find that you want to look one way, but that Venus means your taste and clothing style are different.

So, what does it mean to look like your Ascendant? Let's find out!

ARIES RISING: This Rising appears extroverted right off the bat! Intimidating, even. They're fast and quick and the very first person to dive headfirst into any situation. Of course, all reds look good on them as do all things bold, just like this sign. People with Aries Rising are people of action. They love active sportswear or anything that they can get in and out of super quick. Leave the corsets and thousands of laces to the Capricorns, thank you very much. Ain't no Aries got time for that! Aries rules the head, so all sorts of hats, earrings, bandannas, and glasses are a plus. Expect pronounced brows with a look of determination that projects a fierce energy and a don't-mess-with-me vibe and transmits a seriously tough exterior, even if they are likely softies inside.

TAURUS RISING: Slow and steady, these folks take their time when they first meet people. They may be slow to warm up but they'll get there eventually. They're not in a hurry and radiate chill and serene. Look for a beautiful neck adorned with jewelry or scarves. They have sultry eyes and usually big plump lips. Taurus is ruled by Venus, so they project seduction but are also strong and stable. Stubborn, too. They look fabulous in green. Security is their favorite thing and they loathe change. Most Taurus Risings have a strong physique, much like the Bull. Though they usually vibe more Ferdinand than Pamplona. And no one has a better voice than a Bull Rising.

GEMINI RISING: Quick, adept, and my God do they ever stop talking? This is a curious bunch who excel in communication and make epic flirts. They're nervous and excitable and they'll get you excited too when they really start going. Sprinkle a few good Gemini Ascendants around at your next party. Oh, it'll be a grand time for sure! The majority of Gemini Ascendants are thin and willowy as they merely run on nerves. You can easily spot a Gemini Rising when you see someone talking a lot with their hands and are extra fidgety. They look great in yellow and they love bangle bracelets and rings to emphasize those hands. They prefer comfy shoes too as they actually do like to stand more than sit. And they always have a very lively, alert, and bright look in their eyes.

CANCER RISING: Sweet and sensitive but oh are they moody, Cancer Ascendants change their temperament about every two and a half days, the same amount of time the Moon stays in each sign. At least they're not dull? You can spot a crablike appearance by a strange, rather timid walk, a round Moon-like face, and wide, beautiful eyes. The chest is extra grand and the women prefer low necklines and the men like to show off those pecs. They tend to gravitate toward subtle shades of pale green and blue, but most love silver and navy too. And those eyes! They may be a Cancer Rising signature tale. The eyes will give away their vulnerability. They're amazing nurturers and they are usually excellent chefs. Most love babies and they make fabulous parents. Angelina Jolie, Adele, John Travolta, Mark Wahlberg, and Kate Hudson.

LEO RISING: You'll know when a Leo Rising graces you with their presence. No one in the room can look away. They strut in with their heads held high and a regal air swirling around them. Even the ones who are deeply insecure beam with confidence. Ruled by the Sun, these guys can shine. They sparkle in golds and orange, and their lion's mane is their proudest asset. They're terribly dramatic, which makes them all fabulous actors. They'll out-sing, out-cry, and outshine you on every level. They're competitive and you better give them a big round of applause. Their posture is amazing too. That's the thing about Leo Ascendants—they radiate royalty. No other Rising Sign is as acutely aware of their presence as this placement. They're fantastic dressers. More is more and they actually have wonderful albeit sometimes gaudy taste. Most of them have catlike eyes and insanely large smiles.

VIRGO RISING: Demure and soft, these folks win the prize for "Most Likely to Be Spotted Shopping at Eileen Fisher." Most people see a Virgo Ascendant and assume they've got it all together. That's just a farce, but it's true that Virgo Ascendants really do give off a flawless vibe. They are meticulous in the fashion sense. These guys are snappy dressers with classic taste. They seem intellectual and they usually are! Much like the Gemini Risings, Virgo Ascendants are usually thin from all the worrying they can do. Look for a furrowed brow from all that thinking and an air of natural beauty too. They don't pile on makeup like the Leo Risings. They are big on cleanliness and they want to project a wholesome image. Nothing loud or obnoxious will ever be seen on a Virgo Ascendant. But sometimes they do have a secret side, and it's definitely not as virtuous as you may think. That's the secret of a good Virgo.

LIBRA RISING: The most gorgeous Ascendant is a Libra Rising. Venus-ruled, this is the Ascendant that projects grace, charm, and harmony. They loathe arguments, which makes them prone to people-pleasing and they are difficult not to like. Sometimes that's not such a good thing, though—they want to keep the peace, and will do it at all costs. Most Libra Risings have beautiful and symmetrical features. They love fashion and the arts of all kinds, and wow do they know how to dress! They can be experimental with this and it *still* looks good. The perks of projecting the goddess of beauty, Venus, I guess. You can spot a Libra Rising by the delicate way they handle themselves, the flirtatious smile, and an air of dignity.

SCORPIO RISING: It's easy to spot a Scorpio Rising. Often shy with an intense gaze that bores right through your soul. These guys are *intense* but they don't want you to know it. In fact, they don't want you to know anything about them at all! They're incredibly private when you first meet them. They'll ask a lot about you, but will reveal nothing about themselves. Not until they can trust you. Trust is a stumbling block for a Scorpio Ascendant. They love black—especially black eyeliner. They know their eyes are their most seductive asset. That and their power. And they usually don't want to attract a great deal of attention either. Oh, but no one gives off sexier vibes than a Scorpio Ascendant.

SAGITTARIUS RISING: Here are the optimists of the Ascendant world. They're always smiling, always laughing, and always feeling fine . . . even when they're not, and that's the downside to having a Sag Rising. Even when they're at their lowest, they'll make you think that everything's tip-top! That's why we love them so much. They truly are super crazy upbeat. Sagittarius Ascendants need lots of exercise, they even love looking athletic. To have this Ascendant is to be constantly on the go. There's too much traveling to do! Usually they are very fit, with long faces and pronounced noses. Jupiter-ruled, these guys do everything BIG. They don't mind over-the-top outfits, hair, etc. They somehow get away with it too. Maybe it's all the luck they possess.

CAPRICORN RISING: If you have a Capricorn Rising, you'll never think life was better when you were young. No longing for the glory days here! These guys are usually born into little adults. Type A personalities and high-strung, maybe as a result of hanging around too many adults, or having too many responsibilities when they were little. Don't worry, life gets better for them with age. They even age in reverse! You see, they get more relaxed as time progresses, and it shows. Of course, wherever Capricorn is in our chart is where we are terribly insecure. Cripplingly so. But with time and experience we work it so well, it becomes a great source of pride in the long run. There is no exception with a Cap Rising! That's why Cappy Rising seems so mature. Even way before their years. They usually have a serious look to them and they love to wear black. Some may project melancholy, but it can come off as Goth too. Their bone structure is EPIC.

AQUARIUS RISING: They're so cool and effortless and weird in all the right ways. Or at least they want you to *think* they're weird. First impressions are tough for Aqua Ascendants. They give off detached and frosty vibes and can often come across as bitchy or rude. They don't mean to be, and they are surprisingly loyal once you get past their defense mechanism. Uranus-ruled, these folks are true geniuses, but they often feel as if they're aliens from another world. They're actually really psychic too. Look for a truly individualist, quirky outfit that projects a relaxed and comfortable vibe. Thrift stores are made for you. Aquarius Risings don't compare themselves to everyone so they aren't too concerned with the flock. They are their own personal trendsetter. Zany and unbelievably unique!

PISCES RISING: Intuitive, sensitive, and otherworldly. Pisces Ascendants soak up everything that they come in contact with. Bad vibes are your kryptonite if you possess this Neptune-ruled Ascendant. So best to be super cautious with whom you have around. And people can so easily project onto you too! They'll miss out on ever knowing the *real* you, but their loss. Your ability to become anyone you want to be really works so well in the theatrical sense. Astonishingly artistic and dreamy, Pisces Risings look amazing in long flowy fabrics. Anything that appears as if you're moving underwater. Unsurprisingly, the colors of the sea suit them best, as do metallics of almost any kind. They sometimes look like a fish, with expressive eyes and a slightly open mouth.

LOVE &
ROMANCE

h, love. It is truly a many-splendored thing. It's what makes the world go 'round. All you need is love. Need I go on? But no matter how much we think about it, talk about it, or worry about it, love is still a tricky, tricky thing. We all want that special someone to complete us. There's always that dream person—the partner we think we yearn to be with, who sweeps us off our feet and makes us feel whole. (Or maybe it's just someone who does the dishes every night—everyone is different!) But then there's the kind of person we actually attract. That is, IF we end up with anyone at all.

So how do you determine when you should go looking for love? What kinds of qualities should you be seeking in a significant other? And when you do find your person, when is the best time to get married, or deepen your commitment to one another? And how do you know when it is time to focus on *you* for a while? Never fear, it's all in your astrology chart, my dear. But let's get you up to speed with the basics first.

Romantic relationships begin in the Fifth House. The House of Pleasure gives insight to how we love, how we have fun, and how we behave in our romantic lives. The idea of pleasure can also be strongly correlated with creating, and yes, also creation itself! The Fifth House can touch on things like creative pursuit and culture appreciation, but also the act of procreation, reproduction, and children. Am I enjoying this feeling? Does it make me feel good? Is it bringing me a sense of pleasure? Look for answers to these types of questions here in the Fifth House.

Let's take a look at the chart of the beautiful—and *very* conflicted in the love department—Elizabeth Taylor. Now Liz was no stranger to love. In fact, she herself went through eight, yes, I said EIGHT marriages, so this should be interesting.

Liz's Fifth House is technically empty since there are no planets, although we do find Chiron, the celestial maverick, in there, so she did go about dating quite differently than the rest of us.

CHIRON: Chiron is a small icy body orbiting in our solar system. Is it a comet? An asteroid? That's up for debate— although it's generally considered a comet. What isn't up for debate is how it affects your natal chart. Chiron shines its distant, frozen light on areas of your life that you may find most difficult. But remember, people's biggest weaknesses can also serve as necessary ballast for their greatest strength. Chiron isn't a bringer of bad news, but rather it reveals where we need to focus attention and energy to truly grow and thrive in this life.

But what *sign* did Liz have on her Fifth House cusp? It's Taurus, which means that Venus—the planet of love—was the ruler of her Fifth House. Taylor had her Venus placed right next to Uranus, the planet of shock and surprise and sudden change.

Elizabeth Taylor jumped into dating rather quickly, much to the awe and disapproval of everyone around her. She clearly needed a great deal of variety and excitement in her dating life, and it's an extra added bonus that her love life entertained and jolted her public. I think she loved it all! Elizabeth was a bit of a daredevil when it came to love. But don't think because she had a Taurus in her dating house that a Taurus was what she needed.

Now let's take a peek at Liz's House of Relationships, the Seventh House. The Seventh House reveals the type of marriage you get, and— shockingly—Elizabeth Taylor has an *empty* marriage house! *But, Rachel! you might be saying, how can that be? She was married eight times!!* So let's look to the sign on the cusp of her Seventh House for extra clues. Elizabeth had Gemini here, which means she got bored easily and needed a talkative and curious mate. Gemini is associated with Mercury (the planet that rules communication and curiosity) so that became her default marriage house ruler. Taylor had Mercury right next to her Sun in Pisces and in her Third House of Communication. This furthered her need for an expressive and talkative partner. But look! Elizabeth Taylor had her Mercury opposite the vague and dreamy planet Neptune. A fabulous aid for her acting chops, but an oh so difficult aspect when it comes to marriage. Elizabeth was delusional, idealistic, and full of fantasy with her love life. No wonder she married eight times, and twice to the same person! At some point the spell was broken, and once the honeymoon was over it was back to the Fifth House with no time to waste thanks to crazy Uranus next to Venus.

Ready to try this yourself? Look at your natal chart and find your Seventh House ruler. Study the sign on the cusp, and then go find that ruler. Where your Seventh House ruler is, by sign and by planet is the type of partner you want, then reflect on what brings you pleasure in the Fifth House. In the case of Liz, she was well suited to a talkative Pisces type, perhaps a writer, actor, or teacher of some sort. And, indeed, most of her eight husbands—actors, a producer, a singer, and an attorney—fit this description.

When you start learning to read your chart it's going to be easier to look at each house as a discrete entity, just to get grounded. But remember, the ultimate goal is to regard your chart as an orchestra playing the symphony of your life, rather than a collection of individual instruments.

Take it slow—you don't have to listen to the entire symphony at once! Right now, just work to study the connections between your Fifth, Seventh, and Eighth houses. From those three houses, you'll learn more about where you find fulfillment or experience challenges within the areas of pleasure, children, marriage, relationships, and sex.

WHAT DO YOU NEED
IN A PARTNER?

Sign and planet of Seventh House:

ARIES (Mars is the ruler): Wants a pushy, fiercely protective, and brave mate. Sure you may get an active, aggressive, go-getter type, just watch out for their temper!

TAURUS (Venus is the ruler): Needs someone they can rely on and who makes them feel comfortable. They're looking for a dependable, secure, charming, and sweet type.

GEMINI (Mercury is the ruler): A chatty, intellectual partner suits them best. Someone who is a teacher, writer, speaker, singer. They don't gel with the silent, introspective type.

CANCER (Moon is the ruler): Wants a sensitive, empathic, and nurturing partner. They can be a bit mothering. Just watch out for mothering too much yourself! And they can perhaps be a tad bit moody too.

LEO (Sun is the ruler): A vivacious and showy partner works well if Leo is on your Seventh House cusp. Usually they'll gravitate to someone with a very sunny personality and a wee bit of arrogance.

VIRGO (Mercury is the ruler): A detailed and organized mate lights them up. Someone analytical and sophisticated is the ticket. And if they happen to be a snappy dresser and a hard worker, all the better.

LIBRA (Venus is the ruler): They're looking to marry for love and for companionship. And their mate needs to be beautiful, charming, with the utmost grace.

SCORPIO (Pluto is the ruler): They crave a deeply sensual and sexual relationship with lots of passion and mystery. Intensity is the name of the game!

SAGITTARIUS (Jupiter is the ruler): Desires an optimistic and happy-go-lucky type. Perhaps someone into sports and a general lover of life. A good travel mate and someone who wants to see the world is ideal.

 CAPRICORN (Saturn is the ruler): A moody, loner type turns them on. Sometimes they'll go for older mates too. Honestly, age is really just a number.

 AQUARIUS (Uranus is the ruler): You'll want someone unusual, shocking, and very, very intelligent. You marry for friendship and crave freedom in your relationship too.

 PISCES (Neptune is the ruler): A dreamy, inspired artist, poet, or designer is what you crave. Just make sure they aren't drunken escapists.

EXTRA INSIGHT

Do you have Saturn, Neptune, or Pluto in your Fifth House? You might have some anxiety when it comes to wearing your heart on your sleeve.

Men with a Fifth House Sun often expect their partner to dote on them just like their mama.

Do you see your Moon in your Seventh House? You might hate being alone and partner up just to avoid your fears of loneliness.

Is Chiron in your Seventh House? You have some serious baggage that hinders you from developing close relationships. One of your life tasks is to take risks around being vulnerable and getting rejected.

WHAT TURNS YOU ON?

The Eighth House is where we go to see how we are in bed. Ruled by passionate Mars, the planet of sex and sensuality, it has a lot to say about our libido. The Eighth House is really just *shared energy*, and that's basically what sex is all about. Find what sign is on the cusp of your Eighth House and look below for a quick rundown.

Cancer, Pisces, or Scorpio on the Eighth House cusp are cuddle bugs. They're crazy sensual and are the most touchy-feely signs to have on the sex box.

Unsurprisingly given their emotionally intense nature, and fascination with the darker aspects of life, Scorpio can be a bit twisted and undeniably kinky. Got detached Aquarius here? Sex toys are your thing, as is the occasional ménage à trois. Virgo can seem prudish at first, but it's got a secret sexy side that'll knock your socks off . . . as long as you bathe first. Taurus here means you need to be touched and often! These folks prefer long, sultry, tactile massages and they love a good postcoital meal. Capricorn is slow and cautious, but once they know you are committed, watch out!

Gemini on the Eighth House cusp loves to talk dirty, while Libra is fair in bed. They take turns giving and receiving pleasure.

All the fire signs here are the most playful. Leo, Sagittarius, and Aries are hot-blooded and big fans of strong, passionate sex. Though Leo is the one that really needs an Oscar for their erotic, breathtaking performance. Don't forget the applause!

Does this quickie breakdown sound a lot like your quickies? I thought so! For additional clues look to the placement of Mars and Venus in your chart. Venus is the planet of love and beauty, while you'll remember that Mars is the planet of sex and sensuality. There's a reason we use these symbols for male and female! If you're into women, the placement of Venus in your chart will disclose a thing or two about how you love and what sort of female you're after. If you're into men, check out that Mars to learn what sort of masculine energy sends shivers up your spine.

MARS OR VENUS IN ARIES: Those with a placement here prefer the take-charge types who, unfortunately, may tend to be egomaniacs. Both Mars and Venus in Aries prefer the hunt but lose interest after the object of their desire submits. Aries has zero patience for those who like them back. Yes, this a selfish placement, but the more evolved souls have moved past this. They learn how to keep sex *and* love fresh and wildly unique.

MARS OR VENUS IN TAURUS: These lusty souls take their time when it comes to love and sex. They're also terribly jealous, as they view their love interests as their personal possessions. Both Mars and Venus here go after the well-dressed sort. They love clean-cut fellows, and beautiful women with expensive taste. They crave dependable, stable types and, as an unfortunate side effect, once they find a position or routine they like, they'll do it on repeat.

MARS OR VENUS IN GEMINI: What a flirt! This is a fickle bunch who can change their minds a dozen times before they settle with someone. They go after the intellectuals since what really turns them on is what's between your ears, God bless 'em. But that's not to say they don't have a physical side! You really haven't lived until you've had a full-on make-out session with a Mars or Venus in Gemini. And the moment they moved on, they really do want to remain friends.

MARS OR VENUS IN CANCER: Here are the true romantics. They're sappy too. If they had a good relationship with their parents, they'll go after mates who remind them of their mommies and daddies. Weird, I know, but these guys are loyal, and what they really want is to start a family with you. They prefer their women to be ultra-feminine and the men to be classically masculine. But they're also into aggressive sex. Tie me up, tie me down. They love it!

MARS OR VENUS IN LEO: Treat them like a god, and these folks will love you forever. In truth people with Mars or Venus here go after the show-offs. It's an issue though, as they themselves really need to be the star of the show. They're fabulous in bed as they love a good performance, and their pride is so severe they'll never perform halfheartedly. That is, unless they feel ugly. Mars and Venus MUST feel gorgeous to give their best sexual presentation.

MARS OR VENUS IN VIRGO: To a Mars or Venus in Virgo, sex is simply part of a healthy routine. Much like flossing your teeth, or wearing deodorant. And you better be top-notch with it too if you yourself are after one of these. But please don't let that stop you! These Virgo types love to please and serve. They're turned on by workaholics and health nuts. No one appreciates a toned physique more than them.

MARS OR VENUS IN LIBRA: It's true—beautiful, artistic types arouse those with Mars or Venus in Libra. They're lucky too, as no one is better at courtship than the unflaggingly fair, give-and-take Libras. They know just what to do to charm the pants off their object of desire. All's fair in love and war and it better be equally fair in the bedroom too. They love to give and to get. They make perfect mates, dressed to the nines, and they always smell so nice. You better dress impeccably too if you want a shot at one of these gems.

MARS OR VENUS IN SCORPIO: Sultry, seductive types with or without (preferably with) a sexy foreign accent appeal to those with Mars or Venus in Scorpio. The mystery and the exotic add the allure. Oh, they're amazing in bed. Nothing is too risqué or bizarre. Role playing entices them as does engaging in any fantasy their lucky lovers can dream of. But their partners should be careful not to kiss and tell. Blab about what happens between the sheets, they're outta there for good.

MARS OR VENUS IN SAGITTARIUS: Outdoorsy types and hippies appeal to those with Mars or Venus on Sagittarius. They see love as a sport, so those who fall for them better be ready to play. Sex is fun with them. They're rowdy with lots of laughter and games. Get too serious with these folks, and they'll move on FAST. Keep it light and lively, and always suggest a little quickie in nature too. They *love* that.

MARS OR VENUS IN CAPRICORN: They go for professors, investors, and old souls. They're guarded though, as they've been burned before. But once they take their time and commit, they're incredibly sexual and crazy attentive, but always behind closed doors! Power, money, and fame lure them in. But the more evolved types go for the quiet loners. They love a challenge.

MARS OR VENUS IN AQUARIUS: These folks act like they don't really even need love, but it's not true. This is a frosty bunch who can be surprisingly dynamic in bed. It confuses the rest of us, but to a Mars or Venus in Aquarius, they just need space. They love to shock and awe too, so they have a weird and unusual way of showing love and getting what they want in bed.

MARS OR VENUS IN PISCES: They'll bat their pretty eyes and love to appear a little bit helpless. They love to be dominated in bed and they're even better when they play the helpless victim. It's all an act, as they are the ones that actually want to save you. They go for musicians and artists. Drunks and drug addicts too. If you need help, they'll fall in love. Their fantasy life is probably the most creative of all the signs.

A NOTE ON GIFTS

How do you show your sweetie or the neighbor next door that you care? Sure, you can guess, but if you have their chart, you've already got insta-access into their innermost desires. So why not use it? Look to their Venus or Moon sign to see what it is that they really want. Venus shows their tastes, especially the colors they love. And let's face it, sometimes we just all need to butter up someone every now and then.

ARIES: Whatever you do, don't give them anything vintage. No, they must be the first ones to use it. Better yet, make it something limited edition and ultra-rare. Aries always wants the best. They love diamonds and anything red, black, or white. They love to have their name engraved on things too.

TAURUS: The foodies of the zodiac love to be gifted with fine dining restaurant gift certificates and bottles of bubbly. They have exquisite taste, so they'd rather you get them nothing at all if it isn't expensive, opulent, and luxurious on every level. Textures and fine fabrics excite them. Luscious candles are good too, and all Tauraens love plants.

GEMINI: Give these guys variety and make it FUN. Brightly colored bags packed to the gills with little trinkets and accessories. Oh, and they LOVE bangles, watches, and bracelets and anything that accentuates their expressive hands. Books are a great option too—especially romance novels—because they speak to Gemini's optimism and love of happy endings.

CANCER: Anything vintage or heirloom brings tears to their eyes. Especially if there's a story attached to it. Anything that your grandmother had they will love. Cancers love history, and sentimental gifts are special to them indeed. Just don't forget the card! And you better write more than your name on it!

LEO: Anything ostentatious will do for a Leo. Just whatever you do, make it BIG. Flamboyant wrapping paper with loads of ribbons, cards that sing for you, they even love big yard signs announcing all their accomplishments. Make a fuss. Tell them how young and beautiful they look too. Over and over and over and over and over . . .

VIRGO: These guys love natural gifts from your backyard or even homemade goodies. What they don't want is for you to go out of your way. It embarrasses them, you see. They love the Container Store and a subscription to *Real Simple* magazine. That's the most Virgo magazine I've ever seen.

LIBRA: They love pretty pastels, even the men. They don't care for big or grand, but something sweet and thoughtful touches their hearts. What they really want is to spend the day with you. So take them to a drive-in or a museum. Give them the gift of companionship.

SCORPIO: These passionate souls aren't big into gifts. It's experiences they crave. They love intense adventures like parasailing or cave exploration. For those less risky Scorpios, get them something black, dark red, or blue. A dark candlelit dinner and some risqué lingerie.

SAGITTARIUS: Take them to comedy shows, a sporting event, or a music festival. But while we all wait for normalcy to occur, get them a travel book or take them hiking on your local trail. They love to explore, so a gift from a different country is always a treat. They love bohemian scarves too.

CAPRICORN: Especially if this is their Moon sign, Capricorns are always suspicious when you give them gifts. They think you want something from them, so make sure you let them know why you are gifting them in the first place right away. That way they can enjoy it more. They love black, gray, and white and anything that can be put to good use. Like a new phone case.

AQUARIUS: Gadgets! They love techy things and the newest and most intriguing gizmos. They love electric blues and blinding yellows. Modern things are good and so is anything that benefits a cause. Aquarians are natural humanitarians, so you can always appeal to that.

PISCES: They love music, so a nice wireless speaker or an instrument makes them happy. Art too. A book, a print, or a trip to the museum will do the trick. Pisces are escapists. That's how they celebrate! So pour them a large glass of wine and let them be unrealistic for a day.

FRIENDSHIPS

10

L ove may be what keeps us burning, what charges our yearning souls. But platonic friendship is a balm and key ingredient for a happy, fulfilled life. We need friends and acquaintances to bring out our ideals, ethics, and values and mirror it right back to us. Sharing a cup of tea, or better yet, a cocktail with a friend after a rough week of work is simply one of life's greatest pleasures. Lots of people even view their own personal friend groups as an even more important fixture in their lives than family members (Friendsgiving, anyone?). Astrology can help you understand this oh so pleasant and essential part of your life. When talking about friend groups, it's best to focus on that Eleventh House.

Go find your Eleventh House box on your Astrology Wheel. I'm a good friend—I'll wait! Got any planets in there? This will give you clues to the types of people you need to assist you with your self-development. Now look to the sign on the house cusp. Find the ruler, by sign and by house, to give you extra hints and indications (refer back to page 30 for a quick refresher!).

If the planet in or the planet associated with the sign ruling your Eleventh House is . . .

ARIES OR MARS: You spend a lot of energy on your friendships, attracting brave and energetic types into your own life. You like groups who charge right in, and while they may be of the argumentative or extreme sporty types, there is never a dull moment here.

> **How to piss these friends off:** Become lazy and remain indifferent to their passions.

TAURUS OR VENUS: You crave dependable friends who are stable, predictable, and reliable. You also make a great hostess and attract charming and artistic types into your life.

> **How to piss these friends off:** Mess with all of their stuff, eat all of their food, and never chip in for pizza.

GEMINI OR MERCURY: You have a wide circle of casual friendships who belong to a million different friend groups. You're a social butterfly and you need peeps who spark you on a mental level in a variety of ways. Your phone is always buzzing with updates from the group chat.

> **How to piss these friends off:** Bore them with long, lifeless stories about your feelings.

CANCER OR MOON: Wherever you have Cancer in your chart is where you nurture and mother. So, a Cancer on the cusp of your Eleventh House means you take care of your friends, and if they're good, they'll take care of you right back. You also love to have them over to your home.

> **How to piss these friends off:** Tell them that they're all too emotional and then insult where they live *and* their mothers.

LEO OR SUN: Your friends are show-offs and they probably have good reason to be, so in turn you show them off too! You attract dramatic, theatrical, and a dignified group of folks with impeccable taste. Perhaps you're their leader!

> **How to piss these friends off:** I wouldn't, but if you dare— don't applaud them, then run.

VIRGO OR MERCURY: Your friend group is helpful, well organized, and practical. You don't have a huge friend group, but you are exceedingly loyal to each and every one of them. You'd do anything for them.

> **How to piss these friends off:** Don't bathe and/or interrupt their work schedule.

LIBRA OR VENUS: You cooperate with everyone and you're the person in the group who smooths out conflicts and gets everyone on the same page. You're wildly popular too.

> **How to piss these friends off:** Don't make any decisions and halt all niceties like saying "thank you" and "please."

SCORPIO OR PLUTO: You prefer a small group of friends who vibe deep and introspective. Superficiality turns you off big-time, as depth and mystery are your go-to's via your acquaintances.

> **How to piss these friends off:** Get all up in their business, then tell everyone you know.

SAGITTARIUS OR JUPITER: You have a huge friend circle and adore absolutely everyone. They in turn adore you back, as you're honest and way too much fun. You're a dreamer, and your friends better dream big too. Extra points if they travel with you.

> **How to piss these friends off:** Shatter their dreams with tales of reality, then give them a job to do.

CAPRICORN OR SATURN: You're crazy loyal and friendship is deeply important to you. Why? You've never felt like you've really fit in! So you work extra hard to make sure your friendships are in tip-top shape. Lucky them.

> **How to piss these friends off:** Dial down your ambition and embarrass them in public.

AQUARIUS OR URANUS: Strange and unusual groups of people orbit around you. Fascinating types who are light-years ahead of their time. Oh, they're characters all right, and likely rebellious too. Crusade with them and you'll burn brighter in their company.

> **How to piss these friends off:** Get clingy and text them nonstop. Don't give them any space.

PISCES OR NEPTUNE: Your friend group is made up of artists and musicians. But make sure to select those who are more emotionally evolved to avoid unnecessary drama. These friendships get better with age. You'd give them the shirt off your back.

> **How to piss these friends off:** Tell them their feelings don't matter.

FURRY FRIENDS

Everyone needs a four-legged friend or, at the very least, a little goldfish to call their own. Pets can keep us feeling cheery and loved. Only a loyal critter can still love us when we're at our worst. Unbrushed teeth, hair, and all. Want to learn which pet suits you best? Check out your Sixth House and look to the sign on the Sixth House cusp. This is the health and pet realm and pets are indeed very healthy for us! They lower your blood pressure and your cholesterol. This is also the sector of routine, and unfortunately you'll need a good one for a pet. Otherwise, a pet rock will do quite nicely.

Sixth House Cusp Signs:

ARIES: You're so busy and on the go, you need an energetic pet yourself. Go with Labs, German Shepherds, Corgis, Jack Russell Terriers, and other active sporting dogs. They have just as much stamina as you do.

TAURUS: Any animal that can linger on the couch for long stretches of time is your ideal companion. Cuddly ones are even better. Lazy Basset Hounds are good, as are sluggish, plump, Garfield-like cats. Sloths work too. English Bulldogs and Pugs are also great couch potatoes.

GEMINI: Talkative Gemini gets bored easily with too much silence. Parrots and parakeets are your best friends. But you also do well with yippy Yorkies, Beagles, Chihuahuas, or vocal Siamese cats. Frisky ferrets are also fun and a great conversation starter if you dare to take them for a walk!

CANCER: You're a natural pet parent. And while any dog or cat would be lucky to have you, creatures that retreat into their shells speak to you most. Snails, turtles, hermit crabs, armadillos, and even hedgehogs will suit your style best.

LEO: The lioness sign of Leo on the pet house has a natural affinity for regal felines. But really any flamboyant pet will do. Peacocks, Poodles, Pomeranians, Chow Chows (they LOOK like a lion!), cockatoos, and even lionfish speak to your royal nature.

VIRGO: You appreciate a tidy and hardworking pet. Hairless cats and dogs are good for your allergies, but Border Collies, Boxers, and St. Bernards all possess your amazing and enviable strong work ethic.

LIBRA: You can't stand seeing animals cooped up, so that's a hard pass to anything that requires a tank or a cage. Beautiful social creatures are best for you. Boston Terriers, Pugs, and Beagles are super social and will always help you meet people at the dog park.

SCORPIO: You don't mind the dark side of nature. So, a pet snake that feasts on mice doesn't turn you off one bit. Tarantulas, scorpions, frogs, and lizards—everything your mom was afraid you'd bring home is a good bet. If you do get a dog or cat, make sure they're your favorite color—BLACK.

SAGITTARIUS: You love all dogs. All cats. All creatures. Lazy ones are dull to you, though, as you yourself love to get outside. So active happy dogs like Golden Retrievers, Labs, Siberian Huskies, and Rottweilers are good for you. Horses tug at your heartstrings.

CAPRICORN: Reptiles appeal to your cooler nature. Iguanas and lizards especially. Cats are wonderfully self-sufficient, but if you go for a dog, it needs to be industrious. Hardworking service dogs, like a German Shepherd, would be good for you. Goats too.

AQUARIUS: Strange and unusual pets speak to you. Skunks, sugar gliders, insects, potbellied pigs, and hissing cockroaches, to name a few. But unusual dogs are also appealing. Puli, Chinese Crested, Brussels Griffon, and Pharaoh Hound are as unique as you.

PISCES: Any stray is welcome at your house. One eye or only three legs? Great! You'd save every single living thing if you could. Of course, you also love fish and anything that can swim. You'd pair well with a Portuguese Water Dog, but really, you're not picky.

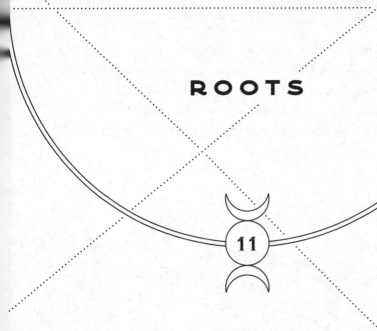

ROOTS

11

Home is where the heart is for a reason. It's our place of safety and refuge. Of course, finding our dream home and the financial reality of being able to live there is a tall, if not impossible, order. But even if cozy Parisian apartments or beach homes in Malibu are out of reach, learning what makes you comfy and secure is important to know, and figuring out how best to achieve that is a key factor in your overall happiness.

The Fourth House represents our home and family life. It's the foundation of our chart and it goes full circle as it discloses what we're like in old age too. Look to the planets in this house for clues of what life was like in your home growing up, and the way you prefer your abode now. Do you gravitate toward a busy, active home? Or do you crave a more quiet and peaceful retreat? As always, look to the planets in the house and of course the sign on the cusp as well.

Equally important in unveiling our relationship to home is the Moon—after all, it is she who determines what it is we *need*. The Moon in astrology discloses our relationship with our mother, reveals how we were nurtured, and how we, in turn, nurture ourselves. If you find the Moon in your Fourth House, it's evidence that you are incredibly caring and resourceful, but you might also be challenged by strong emotions, particularly around things that bring nostalgia. Example time! Let's take a look at the chart of actor and notorious homebody Matthew McConaughey.

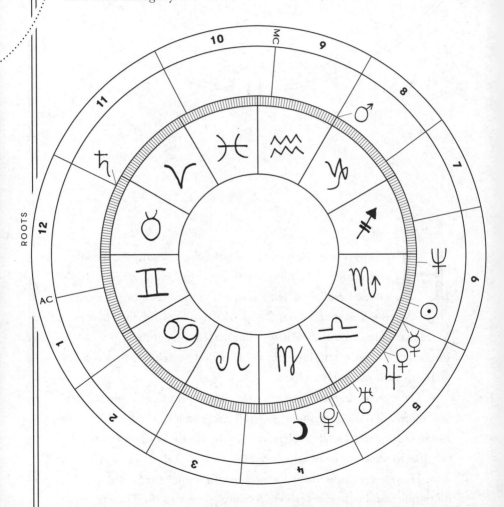

Matthew has the sign of showy Leo on his Fourth House cusp, and he has both Moon and Pluto in his home and family area. Pluto here can indicate lots of transformations and power struggles (which checks out—his parents did apparently divorce twice!). But it's Matthew's Moon in the House of Home and Family that indicates someone who needs his home to recharge.

Security and comfort are HUGE to Matthew. Behind his charismatic and curious Gemini Rising, Matthew is super-sensitive, a classic momma's boy. With a Moon in Virgo, don't be fooled by his carefree, bongo-beating vibe. He's detail-oriented to the extreme. See how his Moon forms a square, or right angle to his Gemini Ascendant? His flirty, quirky persona and his finicky Moon are at odds with one another. What you see is not what you get. Matthew is actually a workaholic with his intense Scorpio Sun in his Sixth House and opposite taskmaster Saturn. This is a beautiful position as he will always want to better himself.

Matthew craves a showy and lavish home with Leo on the cusp of his Fourth House. Of course, he is a successful movie star, so what he wants is what he gets. Take a break one day and check out pictures of his Austin lake villa! Best of all, Matthew will keep getting sweeter with age. He'll have a houseful of grand babies to dote on thanks to Leo and the Moon. And he'll never stop working. The ruler of his Fourth House lies in the work sector.

What sign or planet do YOU have in the Fourth House?

ARIES OR MARS: You're active and independent in your home and with your family. You probably had a take-charge parent, and will probably become the leader of your own household when you yourself have a family. You actually become more energetic as you age, which really just makes the rest of us very, very jealous. You thrive in larger cities with LOTS to do.

TAURUS OR VENUS: Home is a place that needs to be stable and comforting, and yours is probably a beautiful and very tactile place. Filled with gorgeous unique textures and the comfiest of furniture, it's a serene environment. You can hibernate better than anyone and you're destined to become more comfortable and stable as you age. A home in nature is ideal.

GEMINI OR MERCURY: You grew up in a busy, talkative household. Whether it was siblings, friends, family, or just the neighborhood kids coming and going, your childhood home was always full and that's the way you'll prefer your own home too! For those rare moments you're home alone, load your home with puzzles and projects to keep your mind busy. Apartment complexes, busy communities, or even a commune appeal to you.

CANCER OR THE MOON: You really couldn't ask for a better placement than the sign and planet of home and family! You're protective and nurturing and probably had a close-knit and loving home life (or deeply craved that). You're traditional too and may choose to live close to family. No one can create a more welcoming, cozier dwelling than you! Try to live near water if you can help it.

LEO OR SUN: Flamboyant and flashy, your home is meant to impress. You're proud of where you live, but easily become green-eyed and envious. If you can help it, stay far away from Pinterest! Don't worry, you are so creative at home, you can make anywhere a special oasis based on your sheer genius alone! Somewhere warm and sunny makes you happy.

VIRGO OR MERCURY: An organized home is what you crave! This means everything has its place and hell hath no fury like you should anyone you live with fail to keep the order. Oh sure, every Virgo has that one drawer. It's disgusting, but it's your little secret. Tiny homes appeal to you. You need to live in a place where you can walk a lot. It helps keep you calm.

LIBRA OR VENUS: Well, isn't your home a beautiful place! You have an eye for elegance and grace, and you prefer a household that radiates peace and harmony. If there's the slightest bit of chaos in your home, however, you instantly move to stress. You love to live in upscale places that radiate the same good taste you do.

SCORPIO OR PLUTO: You're ultra-private about home and family matters—protective too! Your family secrets run deep, but so does your loyalty. I pity the fool who lashes out at *your* family members. Scorpio is the sign of transformations, so expect lots of shifts in your home throughout your lifetime. You prefer a hidden escape.

SAGITTARIUS OR JUPITER: You have a raucous home life! It's a fun and entertaining place and you're oh so generous with it too. Of course, you may not be at home much as you love to see the world and explore. Freedom is big and you probably live in a faraway place, or at least further away from where you grew up. Not that home life was bad, far from it. You just crave different perspectives. Anywhere with easy access to an airport is a good bet for you.

CAPRICORN OR SATURN: Growing up might not have been so warm and fuzzy. That's okay. You develop stronger family ties the older you get. Traditions are big to you too, and your home aesthetic is refined, classy, and extremely sophisticated. Basically, you have superior taste. Security and stability is something you strive for, and you'll get it too. You don't mind colder climates or someplace gloomy like London or Seattle.

AQUARIUS OR URANUS: Your home is weird and unusual and a little bit bizarre. You usually don't compare yourself to the Joneses as you strive to be wildly different. No cookie-cutter McMansion for you! You need space and freedom as you hate to be tied down. Perhaps you move around a lot, but you never feel as if you're "settled." One of your parents was odd or just plain crazy. And you yourself get stranger and more innovative the older you get. You crave a home that has loads of space and lots of technology.

PISCES OR NEPTUNE: Ethereal and dreamy describes your abode. It's your own private sanctuary and escape! If you didn't grow up in an artistic home, you probably felt a bit disconnected from your family somehow. You crave blues and greens and do well if you can live near water. At the very least a kiddie pool will do! You become more compassionate and psychic as you get older.

ASTROCARTOGRAPHY   There's an entire sect of astrology discovered by the late Jim Lewis called Astrocartography or Astrolocality. It's basically the map of the world aligned with your personal natal chart and it'll show you the best places to live and the not so great places to visit. You can find your own Astrocartography chart on astro.com. People do very well when they move close to their Sun, Jupiter, Venus, or Mercury line. Saturn is a tough one. It means you work a lot, but some people are cool with that. Full disclosure, I myself reside on a Saturn line. When one locates to their Pluto line, great shifts and transformations occur. Be careful with that one. Moving to your Mars line brings a strong warrior-like energy into that place. You're courageous but also ready for a fight. It can get exhausting after a while. A Neptune line can become a great vacation spot. It's the planet of escape! But be careful living on your Neptune line alone. Reality can be so hard.

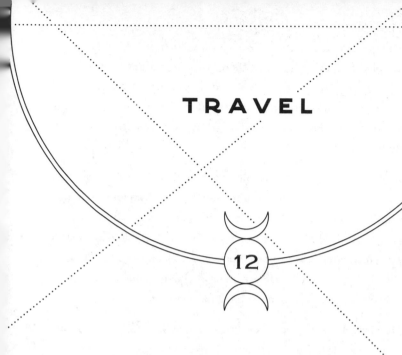

TRAVEL

12

We've taken a look at where you are best suited to live, but what about when you want to hit the road? Everyone needs a break every now and then and getting to spend time in new places can broaden our horizons and change our point of view. It shifts our attitude and puts our own sometimes silly little problems into some much needed perspective. Of course, some people loathe the very idea of travel! They freak at the notion of boarding a plane, or sailing down the interstate at mach speed. Their idea of recharging is staying at home and getting around to a thousand to-do's, thank you very much. But for the rest of us, we look to our Ninth House to see where our own wanderlust resides. It's the house where we see the Big Picture and a good holiday will afford us just that.

The Fifth House should be taken into consideration too. That's the house where we find out what's fun and how we like to celebrate—which I for one think is a pretty big component when considering a vacation—but for now, let's just focus on that Ninth House. Of course, planets in the Ninth make a big impact on your travel destination too. For example, if you've got Venus there, you need a gorgeous destination or you'll get depressed. Saturn here might mean you only travel for work, and if you've got weird and wild Uranus here, unusual and unconventional locales are your thing. Don't forget Astrocartography can help too!

ARIES: Stodgy tour buses and slow-paced sightseeing excursions bore you to tears. You need action! Excitement! The freedom to roam at will! You're impulsive with your travel plans and prefer spontaneous, fly-by-the-seat-of-your-pants traveling. Routines and schedules make you crazy. You crave adventurous jaunts like zip lining in Costa Rica, horseback riding in Jackson Hole, and hiking in Peru. Any place that keeps you active and on the move is the place for you.

TAURUS: Travel isn't fun unless it's flecked with banquets of luxurious cuisine and fine wine. Gastrotourism was designed specially for you. Your idea of unwinding includes lots of massages, shopping, and oh, did we mention food? You also love nature, but not in any extreme way like an Aries would. A sustainable farm-to-table expedition would do nicely, as would pastries in Paris, oysters in New Orleans, tapas in Barcelona, or pasta in Tuscany. You're a true epicurean!

GEMINI: You're so good at different languages, any foreign destination means you get to show off your brilliant verbal skills. You're restless too, so walkable cities filled to the brim with museums ignite your curiosity and never-ending quest for knowledge. You're also not one to shy away from day trips, even if you spent twenty-six hours just to get to your destination. Barcelona, Tokyo, Cairo, London, and Athens are all good for you.

CANCER: Get thee to water and fast! You love any destination near it. You also love to bring family on your travels too. Nothing like a good old-fashioned bonding experience, right? Islands that are relaxing and comfortable are your go-to. Cancer is more a traditional sign that doesn't like to take too many risks. Safety, security, and assurance are big when you finally do decide to leave your precious home. Vienna,

Bora Bora, Hawaii, Martha's Vineyard, Iceland, and Niagara Falls all light up your soul.

LEO: You love a good party and any place that sports beautiful, sunny beaches. You're a Sun God! But the nightlife must be grand too, as you've got closets full of gorgeous costumes that are meant to be shown off! And please, no coach or economy class for you. It's first class all the way, baby! And a place where the action is has you intrigued. Barcelona, Dubai, Buenos Aires, and the South of France all live up to your high travel standards.

VIRGO: Practical and very, very plan-oriented, you need a well-organized vacay with lots of activities for that overactive mind. Virgo is associated with health so any wellness retreat is epic for you. But look out for an oversensitive stomach, so stay away from any greasy or overindulgent foods. Places like Ojo in Santa Fe, Miraval Spa and Resort, Desert Hot Springs California, or Rancho La Puerta in Mexico would be a good fit.

LIBRA: Romantic vacations are your absolute favorite as you never truly like to travel alone. Beauty and symmetry are also big on your agenda, so exquisite cities and gorgeous natural retreats are where you want to flock when needing to recharge. Prague and Croatia are stunning and elegant enough to fit the bill. More nature-oriented spots like Napa Valley or Banff National Park can be stunning too, with natural settings that are refined enough to meet your breathtaking qualifications.

SCORPIO: You never want to be dependent when you travel. Reliance on transportation or staying in other people's homes only irks and disrupts your style. It takes away your power and you hate that. Walkable cities and the freedom to dictate your own schedule appeal to you as does anything old, historic, and worn. Ruins are especially your thing. Tulum, Athens, Pompeii, and Machu Picchu are all great spots for you.

SAGITTARIUS: The sign of travel in the house of travel isn't too picky about jaunting off on a whim to anywhere in the world. Here are the adventurous eaters and reckless tourists, the more daring the better! You don't care particularly how many stars your hotel has as long as it's in a fascinating place. India, Thailand, Hong Kong are just a few items on your bucket list. Honestly, you've probably conquered them all!

CAPRICORN: You appreciate elegance and style. You also believe that you get what you pay for, so you're not one to cash in on any discount vacation or Groupon special. You are pure class, and your travel spot must reflect your seriously high standards. Cold weather doesn't deter you either. St. Petersburg (Russia, not Florida), Istanbul, Vancouver, and London are all great places for you. Just give yourself plenty of time. It takes Capricorn a bit longer to unwind.

AQUARIUS: Unconventional travel destinations are what you love. No Disney World for you! You need a place that is odd and extraordinary. Someplace that is almost the exact opposite of where you live, so you can experience a true change. You're a nonconformist and your travel destinations need to have a unique and oddball vibe as well. The Tianzi Mountains in China, the Bermuda Triangle, and the Catacombs of Paris are all as unique as you are.

PISCES: You prefer the sea anywhere you go. And you can't bear seeing too many homeless people or stray dogs. It breaks your heart when you can't save everyone, I know. You crave whimsical and magical destinations. New Orleans for Mardi Gras, Ireland, Belize, or the Oregon coast are all special places for you.

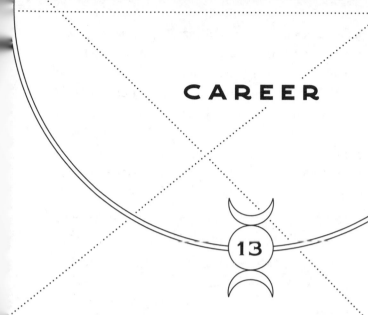

CAREER

13

When we're not going wild with throw pillows at home or sailing the seven seas, we can probably be found at work. Having a satisfying work life is one of the greatest gifts you can give yourself and your astrology chart will absolutely tell you the best way to make your mark in the world. Whether that be in an executive position or as a stay-at-home parent—a mighty fine and difficult job indeed. Our chart discloses what makes our souls sing and what we need to feel safe and secure, all things that must be taken into healthy consideration while finding a career that suits us best. For instance, if you have your Sun in the travel-oriented Ninth House, and your Moon in the creative Fifth House, a boring old desk job might be the start of a soul-crushing depression. Sorting out our strengths and weaknesses helps us in finding our true bliss, something that everyone wants!

The Tenth House in astrology, the Midheaven—or career house cusp, is THE cosmic indicator that reveals how we thrive in the outside world. It indicates our public persona and our social standing and represents our reputation, achievements, and worldly success. The Midheaven stands for Medium Coeli (MC), which is Latin for "middle of the sky." For example, if you were born around lunch, then your Sun sits near your Midheaven when the Sun is at its highest position. And the Tenth House is basically just that. It's where we shine in the world.

Of course, it's also what we aspire to be. It takes work, schooling, mentoring, and a great deal of experience to reach that peak in our own chart. So don't fret if you haven't yet achieved everything you want! This is the stuff of a lifetime and requires plenty of time, patience, and sometimes just good ol' fashioned luck. Let's take a look again at the chart of former president Barack Obama.

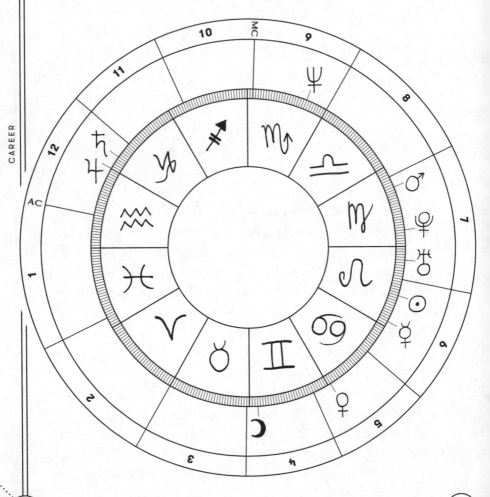

Obama has an *empty* Tenth House. His MC is in the sign of Scorpio, which means it's his basic career path to heal and transform. Because there are no planets in this house, Pluto, the planet aligned with the Tenth House, becomes the ruler of his career house. Obama's Pluto can be found in the Seventh House of Relationships. So, working with and for people is where Barack shines. It also indicates that whoever he marries will be an equally important component in his career. Plus it's Uranus, that shocking planet that dares to be different, that is making a tight square aspect to his MC. And as the FIRST black president in history, he definitely made a distinct mark.

Now go find your own MC. Got any planets in that Tenth House too? Great! Take a look to see what YOU want to reach your highest goals. Don't forget to find your career house *ruler*. This will help determine and shape where you excel, by sign and by house. For example:

ARIES MC: You're a pioneer! You want to be the first AND the best at what you do. You're crazy competitive and always have energy for your career. You're courageous, determined, and great at starting new projects. You may argue with your boss, though, and you can't stand being told what to do. Look to the planet Mars for more clues, but generally speaking Aries MC is an innovative placement that wants to stand out from the crowd. They are fabulous self-starters.

TAURUS MC: Your career path is slow and steady. You need something secure and reliable, and all Taurus MCs are fabulous with money. Taurus is ruled by Venus so working in the arts is always a plus. Averse to change, once you find your ideal job you'll do your best to stick it out.

GEMINI MC: Multitaskers, the lot of you! You excel at writing, singing, speaking, and communication of all kinds. You're amazing at sussing out trends and you thrive in adaptable and fast-paced environments. Gemini is associated with the Twins, so often Gemini MCers have two careers going at once.

CANCER MC: You nurture your career, and you have a compassionate nature that shines through in whatever you choose to do. Most of you would do well in industries like food, clothing, or housing. You also excel with children and assisting people in general. Any career where you can use that famous intuition works well for you.

LEO MC: You LOVE to be onstage and are a natural performer. Courageous and highly creative, any vocation that puts you in the spotlight is good for you. Even if the rest of the chart is shy and reclusive, you excel in a high-profile position. You need attention and applause, but watch your ego—other people need a standing ovation at times too.

VIRGO MC: You're meticulous and strategic with your career. Routine and structure is crucial to you, but watch out for nitpicking everyone else at work. Perfectionism can at times be your worst enemy. You would excel in any area of health or wellness, especially bodywork like massage, physical therapy, or acupuncture. Teaching and science are also good.

LIBRA MC: You strive for balance in your career, which automatically makes you a great manager, mediator, counselor, or lawyer. Everything must be fair and just. Libra also thrives in the beauty industry and they do well in business partnerships of all kinds.

SCORPIO MC: Scorpio is the sign of transformation, so you may go through quite a few of those in your career if you have this Midheaven. In general Scorpio Midheavens are epic investigators, healers, doctors, and therapists. You guys go to the darker places of humanity with no problem at all, and we're all grateful for it!

SAGITTARIUS MC: You need freedom in your job! A career that ignites your desire to explore and travel (well, maybe we'll get there again) is good for you. You also make an excellent teacher and philosopher. It's a nightmare for you to be constantly trapped indoors, so a job that has you moving around a lot is your best bet.

CAPRICORN MC: You're a natural entrepreneur, but you thrive in traditional work environments that promote structure and routine. Success is important to you, and you get it when you have your

Midheaven here. This is hands down the most ambitious of all the MCs. Each and every one of you has the ability to make it to the top.

AQUARIUS MC: Another MC that needs freedom. In fact, the majority of you should be self-employed as you guys make *terrible* employees. You can't tolerate authority! It's also quite common for Aqua MCs to change their careers on a whim. All of you are beautifully inventive and are fabulous with all forms of technology. Weird and unusual careers suit you best.

PISCES MC: Having the sign of Pisces here can make your career decision vague during the early part of your life. But all Pisces MCs are highly intuitive in their careers. Artists, musicians, and actors make up the vast majority of careers. Spiritual and healing vocations are wonderful too. Check out where Neptune is in your chart for more insight into your specific gifts, but this is a very creative placement!

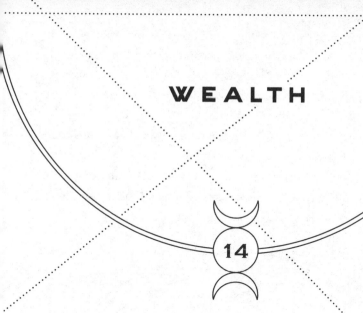

WEALTH

14

Having a job we love is essential but let's face it, money makes the world go 'round—or so they say. One thing's for sure, we all need it and we all *think* we could do with a little more of it. Though that's a topic for another day, there's no question that a cushy lifestyle affords us freedom, much needed peace of mind, and not to mention a few treats to fill that void every now and then. Money especially weighs on our minds in a time when Uranus—the planet of sudden and extreme change—is in the money-ruled sign of Taurus. At such a time, there is money to be made—and fortunes to be lost. Change can be scary but it's also part of life. If we can remain nimble and open-minded, we're more likely to come out on top.

Of course, your chart will tell you *your* attitude toward the green stuff and the best way to get it too. The Second and Eighth houses are known as the money sectors and finding the ruler of your money house is key to your personal stock market. The Second House can illuminate your personal finances, your values, and your self-worth, while the

Eighth House reveals your relationship to other people's money, what you accumulate through marriage, family, and partnerships. There are other factors to look at as well. Venus is also associated with money, and locating Jupiter in your chart will disclose where you are lucky and expansive.

However, when it comes to money, more is always better. Amirite? Transits and progression are super revealing and it might be worth consulting a really good astrologer who can help you figure things out. Better yet, find a FINANCIAL astrologer. Meanwhile, let's take a look at the chart of mega-business tycoon Warren Buffett.

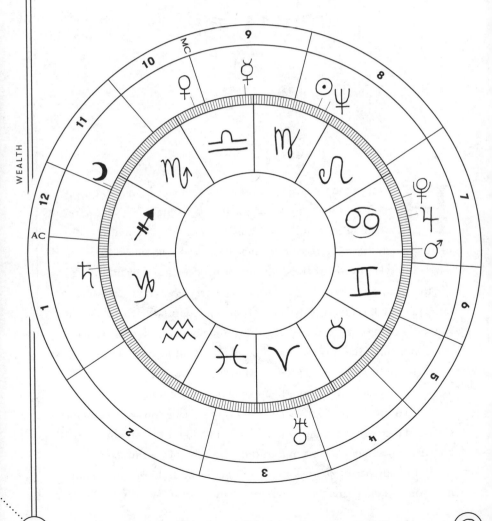

Warren is the chairman and CEO of Berkshire Hathaway. His claim to fame is becoming one of the wealthiest people in the world, but it's his low-key lifestyle and frugal attitude toward his finances that interest me most. Take a look at Warren's Second House. The house of personal income is shockingly empty. And he has Aquarius on his money box, which means Uranus is his Money House ruler. Wherever we have Aquarius in our chart is where we march to the beat of our own drum, and that's exactly what Warren does. Remember that Aquarius is a philanthropic sign, so it comes as little surprise that Warren is a notorious do-gooder. His Moon in Sag also wants this world to be a better place! Aquarius in our chart is where we can detach. No wonder Warren prefers to roam in Nebraska and live out a more prudent lifestyle. Freedom from money is HUGE to him. Probably his secret to success. It absolutely does not control him.

Uranus, his Money House ruler, sits in the Third House of Communication opposite Venus and his Midheaven (even more detachment!), so he makes shocking and brilliant career decisions. But it's his Virgo Sun near Neptune in his capitalist house that has me most intrigued. Sure the Sun in the Eighth gives him natural moneymaking abilities, but Neptune? Neptune is the planet of illusions and dreams. It can be very, very psychic or extremely escapist. A fascinating find! Warren has been nicknamed the "Oracle" for his savvy and uncannily intuitive abilities with all things financial. The fact that both his Sun and Neptune are brilliantly aspected by the hardworking Saturn in Capricorn only aids his dazzling business persona.

Let's look at a contrasting example, TV personality Kylie Jenner. As of the writing of this book, Jenner is worth a whopping $700 million. Not too shabby, eh?

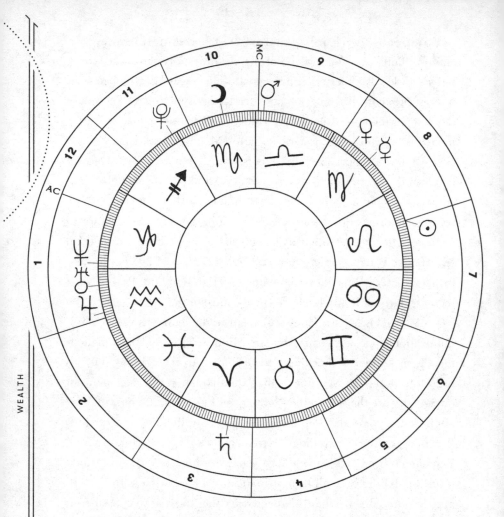

Like Buffett, Kylie also has her Sun in the Eighth House AND an empty Money House with Aquarius on the cusp. But Kylie's Moon in Scorpio wants fame and notoriety and her insecure Capricorn Rising pressures her to be so prosperous. Success IS the best form of revenge after all, would you not agree? Kylie's super smart too: Her Mercury and Venus are in the meticulous sign of Virgo and in the money realm. Her Money House ruler sits in the First House and that makes sense because it's her image that brings in the dollars. Interesting that Libra is her MC too. Although Kylie is blessed (or cursed?) to be born into such a prosperous family, she really came into her own after she launched her cosmetic line. Très Libra, don't ya think?

Shall we consider one more example? Because, truly, how can we resist diving into the chart of Nicolas Cage? It's well known that Nicolas has had his fair share of money problems. Not making it, of course—the guy is loaded. It's just the holding on to it that is so difficult.

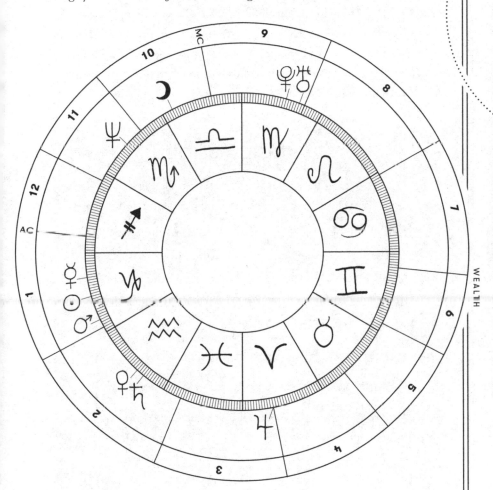

Besides purchasing a castle, an island, and a dinosaur skull, Ol' Nic even blew $150K on a pet octopus. (That's almost $20,000 a tentacle!) Nicolas has Capricorn on the cusp of his Money House, along with fearful Saturn next to Venus. Just having Saturn and Capricorn here alone means money terrifies him. Usually these people are good with money, as their biggest fear is not having security, but Nic has his

Saturn and Venus squared by Neptune and that, my friends, is where the problem resides. Neptune can be completely delusional or highly inspired. Sometimes even both! So, how do you think Nic uses *his* Neptune? Thank goodness the ruler of his Money House is also in trine with his Libra Moon in the career house. He's lucky with opportunities.

One thing Warren, Kylie, and Nic show is that there are a lot of ways to make money and spend it too. And they can all be deciphered in your natal chart. But enough from me, I'm off to purchase a cephalopod with my book advance!

PRACTICE SESSION!

Look at your different planets (and where they are on your chart) for cues on your personal prosperity and abundance.

VENUS reveals what things you attract and how you might best earn the green stuff.

MARS reveals your energy and stamina to chase abundance.

JUPITER reveals where you might find luck.

SATURN reveals longer-term stability, investments.

URANUS reveals the roller coaster of ups and downs with your prosperity.

NEPTUNE reveals your dreams and schemes.

PLUTO reveals big extremes, big money, and big business.

WELLNESS & BALANCE

15

I see lots of people who come to astrologers to learn more about their personal health, or ways they can enrich their self-care to face challenging seasons in their lives. You might not expect it, but those celestial bodies have a lot to say about our physical bodies. In fact, each sign in astrology is also associated with a part of the body:

Aries: head, face, sinuses, brain, eyes, skull, ears

Taurus: throat, tonsils, larynx, mouth, thyroid, vagus nerve

Gemini: lungs, respiratory system, allergies, nervous system, arms, lungs

Cancer: stomach, breasts, digestive system, bodily fluids, uterus

Leo: heart, circulatory system, spine, major arteries

Virgo: intestines, food assimilation

Libra: kidneys, skin, female sex organs, adrenal glands

Scorpio: male sex organs, eliminative system

Sagittarius: hips, thighs, loins, sciatic nerve, liver

Capricorn: bones, back, knees, joints, teeth

Aquarius: shins, calves, ankles, Achilles tendon

Pisces: feet, lymphatic system

MEDICAL ASTROLOGY has been around for eons and the actual name for it is iatromathematics. Of course, we've come a long way from leeches and bloodlettings, baby. Nothing beats those MDs! But what astrology is grand with is TIMING. You can determine when your defenses are down and when you're more prone to an illness. Fantastic information, if you ask me. And if you need surgery, make sure not to schedule it when the Moon in the sky isn't in the same sign that rules that part of the body. For example, just say no to an elective surgery on your boobs when the Moon is in Cancer. It rules the breasts, you see. The Moon in general needs to be watched as well. Full Moons are notoriously more difficult to recover under, while New Moons are best. Though don't let it stop you if you are in a real emergency—which is probably showing up in your chart anyway.

Technically, we look to the Sixth House for all things health and wellness—that house rules our routines, and one can't truly be in good health without a proper routine (though I know many Sagittarians who would disagree) so be sure to consult that house as well.

But looking to the Sixth House is really great at discovering the best way to take care of yourself. For instance, let's say you have warrior Aries on the cusp of the Sixth House. This means your workout regime is very yang-oriented, so you'd do well with CrossFit, Ninja Warrior, or training for obstacle races like a Spartan. Pisces on the Sixth House cusp needs a more gentle routine, like swimming or yoga. And if you've got Aquarius on the health house, you'll gravitate more toward alternative medicine and all things New Age in terms of health and exercise.

When I'm doing a reading, I also look to the First House and that Ascendant. The First House is our physical body, after all! Stressed-out Leo Risings usually get back pain. While Gemini Ascendants get allergies when they aren't at their best. But it's really the Moon that is my go-to when it comes to health. We need that Moon to keep us balanced. If we don't give ourselves what we psychically and emotionally *need*, we get stressed and sick. It can be psychosomatic for sure, but the Moon is a crucial player in the realm of all things healthy.

Understanding our Moon is the best way to learn how to nourish yourself. It'll reveal the style in which you need things. Moon in Taurus means you're patient with your needs, in contrast to now, now, NOW Aries. Of course, the house in which your Moon inhabits is also critical. Your Moon might crave balance and fairness in Libra, but if it also sits in the Second House, you need money, honey.

Now, naturally, if you focus exclusively on your Moon, you'll throw yourself all out of whack. Too much emphasis on that Moon means you're not addressing the needs of your Sun, or your soul's mission in this lifetime. Do not neglect it! But it feels oh so good to indulge in that Moon.

Moon signs:

ARIES MOON OR MOON IN THE FIRST HOUSE: This is the most impatient Moon of the bunch! The most chivalrous Moon too. These folks want to fight and they'll fight for you. Crusaders, all of them. It's true what they say, grass never grows under an Aries Moon's feet. Here are the ones that are constantly in motion—they even eat on the move! Their passion runs high, and these guys have burning desires that they want met NOW. Patience is not their strong suit. They're great at starting things too. They'll leap into action, all guns blazing, but rarely do they finish what they start. That's where the rest of us come in. Moon in Aries is a pioneer. They want to be first and they need to be the best. They're crazy fast with everything and they'll do better when they slow down and take their time . . . if they can stand it!

TAURUS MOON OR MOON IN THE SECOND HOUSE: Taurus Moon needs security—money too. A Taurus Moon is an exalted Moon, which is just a fancy way of saying it's a very stable Moon to have. It's hard to shock people when they have their Moon here. They're like rocks, all of 'em. They make fabulous listeners and you can tell them absolutely anything. They won't seem surprised, or taken aback, or even the slightest bit judgey. This is why so many of them make great confidants. They crave the comforts of life. A big, beautiful meal, fine wine, and the most epic couch of all time. It is actually fun for a Taurus Moon to get horizontal for weeks on end! A little TV, a big bowl of carbs. This is BLISS. The late Debbi Kempton-Smith said the symbol of Taurus should be a baked potato instead of a Bull. They do love the comforts of life . . . and good music. A lot of them have beautiful voices, which can turn shrill and high-pitched if you mess with their stuff. They all love their possessions.

GEMINI MOON OR MOON IN THE THIRD HOUSE: What does a Gemini Moon need? To talk. A lot. A lack of communication makes these guys depressed. They're happiest when they are learning. They process information so damn quickly too. They're basically smarty-pants with a big mouth. They excel in writing, teaching, talking. They hate staying in. They need to travel around and remain in almost constant motion, all the while picking up bits of info here and there and ready to pass it on to the rest of us. They love to be current on all things. They keep us current too! Good luck on keeping up with them. Though they'll love you if you do. Here are an inquisitive bunch who secretly love trashy reality shows, as they are generally curious how the rest of us live our lives. You see, these guys need people. Sure, they can be awful gossips, but they never mean to be cruel. They're just passing along information!

CANCER MOON OR MOON IN THE FOURTH HOUSE:
Sentimental and deeply affectionate, this is the best place to have your Moon, as the Moon is in its home in the sign of lunar-ruled Cancer. This is a feminine Moon that runs on feelings. Mushy feelings too. Cancer Moons are crazy clingy, they cling to people and to the past.

They'll never forget that one time you hurt their feelings way back in 1992. They won't let you forget it either. It's important for people with a Cancer Moon to learn to let go, at the very least for their own psyche if not for everybody else. Family and home are everything to these Moons, and they make wonderful parents. They dote on babies and children and in general work well with kids. Yes, they're sappy, but true sweeties.

LEO MOON OR MOON IN THE FIFTH HOUSE: This is the most childlike Moon of the group! No one, and I mean NO ONE can throw a temper tantrum like someone with a Moon in Leo. You'd better flatter, applaud, and laugh at all their jokes if you want to avoid their ire. They have superb taste and their needs better be met or look out! They simply have standards, you see. This is a dramatic Moon. Theatrical and regal. Insanely creative too and talented beyond belief, and boy can they bring the drama! It's fun to be in the presence of a Leo Moon. They're constantly onstage and deep down they want to entertain you. They say they're good with kids, but maybe it's because at their core, they truly are a kid themselves. But when they are good, they're dignified and golden. Inspiring, as well. They need art in their lives and loads of creative projects as well. It keeps the drama to a minimum and that's good. Life without a Leo Moon is a very dull life indeed.

VIRGO MOON OR MOON IN THE SIXTH HOUSE: Warriors, but sensitive too. Here are the Moons with stomach issues and sensitivities. It's all that neurosis they so easily possess. Good luck getting them to calm down, but it can be done! It's exercise they need. That, and a grand ol' cleaning routine. They love lots of baths and showers and good fresh clean clothes. Housecleaning is good for their soul too. The less clutter they see, the calmer they become. Nature is grand for them and they know it. City life is too much for them and they need breaks. They also need a journal. Getting their brains on paper helps them in SO many ways. They're prone to OCD tendencies, so let them fuss. Work is good for them. Virgo Moons are natural busy bees. They'll never stop coming up with stuff to do and work on. Secretly, they love it.

LIBRA MOON OR MOON IN THE SEVENTH HOUSE: Balance and equality are the emotional go-to here. Fairness too. They crumble if they live in an argumentative household since they thrive on peace, and heaps of it. But what is it they really want? A partner! This Moon needs a companion at almost all times. They really do hate to be alone. It doesn't always need to be romantic either, but that's what Libra Moons do best! No other Moon pays as much attention to YOU as this Moon does. They dote, they bat their eyelashes, and they listen. They excel in working people to their advantage, but they're even better at making you think it was your idea. Oh, they're sneakier than you think. But their charm and grace are so compelling and so beautifully executed, who cares?

SCORPIO MOON OR MOON IN THE EIGHTH HOUSE: This is a secretive and powerful Moon to possess. These guys feel everything deeply, and even more so when they were young. They sensed others didn't have the emotional depth they did, so they learned to stuff it down. Way down. Particularly the men. But as they grow and go through life, they learn to give in to their vulnerabilities. They simply hate feeling out of control. The smart ones realize control is simply a mirage. Their feelings are more powerful than most and that's their real fear. They know a thing or two about power, and they love to play the detective and learn about psychology. They do well in a crisis situation and no other Moon can keep a secret like they can. No other Moon can go for the jugular like they can either. They're psychic, you see. And they can find your weak spot in no time flat.

SAGITTARIUS MOON OR MOON IN THE NINTH HOUSE:
Responsibility may not be their strong suit, but man are these guys FUN. Sag Moons will have you cracking up and doubled over when they really get going. No other Moon is as optimistic, buoyant, confident, or as jolly as them. And they're equally generous. Forget the shirt off their back, they'll give you their last cookie or beer. They have their dark days, but it never lasts long. On the off chance they are feeling blue, take them to a new place. They love to travel and see the world. It's their favorite thing to do.

CAPRICORN MOON OR MOON IN THE TENTH HOUSE: The most ambitious Moon to have. This Moon needs to work but not just for work's sake. Oh no. They really don't want you to know it, but it's fame and recognition they seek, even though they'll never act showy like a Leo Moon would. They're subtle and cautious with their needs. Calculating too. No other Moon has access to such amazing self-discipline like a Capricorn Moon does. They are responsible, rational, efficient, and shrewd. Most with this Moon possessed mothers who were similar in this way. Strict and cold is how they were nurtured and it's the way they prefer to nurture themselves right back. They're funny too, in the sarcastic sense. Dry humor is where they really excel.

AQUARIUS MOON OR MOON IN THE ELEVENTH HOUSE: They need people, and lots of 'em! They love you when you're eccentric, eclectic, and just plain odd. It makes them feel better, as they're super odd deep down themselves. Their feelings seem to come out of nowhere, and they're not great at dealing with feelings. What they do excel in is dreams. They need a goal and an aspiration. Without a wish to reach for, these guys get blue. Help them find theirs and they'll *really* love you. They see friendship in everyone—their moms, the postman, their dentist. Even their lovers are true friends at heart. Funny how these Moons can get so detached, yet be so undeniably loyal. But they are weirdos at heart and that's why we love them.

PISCES MOON OR MOON IN THE TWELFTH HOUSE: Here are the sensitive souls. Their antennas are receptive beyond belief, and my God, are they *psychic!* A good Pisces Moon doesn't miss a thing. These are secretive Moons too. Sometimes they don't know themselves very well. Too busy trying to merge with everyone else, perhaps. But more than likely, they're trying to save everyone. Animals too. Don't tell them too much bad news. They take it on and it mucks up their impressionable auras. This is why the lower-evolved Pisces Moons are so good at becoming the victim. They blame everyone else for their troubles, and maybe it's true. But the good ones know just how strong they are.

SPIRITUALITY & PSYCHIC ABILITIES

16

I 'm someone who believes we're all a little bit psychic. Every one of us has access to our intuitive Moon, spiritual Neptune, and deeply instinctive Pluto. Of course, it's that brain of ours that is constantly questioning *everything*. Our mind is what stands between us and a pure sense of our intuition. Looking at you, Virgos! And anyone else with a Gemini/Virgo Moon, Sun, Rising, or Mercury. And you peeps with Mars in the Third or Sixth House—classic worriers and overthinkers all of you. Not always such a bad thing, but when it comes to sussing out what the universe is trying to tell us, our brain is often-times not our friend.

Meditation is a grand tool that can help each and every one of us to slow down and listen to our instincts. And learning the I Ching, tarot, and especially astrology can become incredibly helpful as we journey down the path of discovering and opening to our own psychic abilities.

The psychic houses are the Fourth, Eighth, and Twelfth. These are all the water sign sectors (Cancer, Scorpio, and Pisces), and if you've got any personal planets in any of these realms or signs, you have a natural skill set in the intuitive department.

But what is it that renders some more pyschic than others? Let's take a look at some famous sensitive people to see what makes them super intuitive.

First on the list is the late renowned psychic Sylvia Browne. Sylvia was born with her Sun in Libra, Moon in Sag, and an eclectic Aquarius Rising. Her Sun was located in the very deep and psychic Eighth House. This means Sylvia thrived in the realm of transformation and death—after all, she did claim that she communicated with ghosts! She excelled in crisis situations and was more of a therapist and healer with

Midheaven (career cusp) in Scorpio. Her Moon, however, in freedom-seeking Sag in the Tenth House, *needed* fame and recognition. It's an added bonus that her Venus was conjunct with her Midheaven, indicating how charming and charismatic she was in her job. But check out that ruler-of-chart Uranus. Since Sylvia had Aquarius Rising, this renders Uranus the ruler of the chart, and she had it placed in the communication house and in a gorgeous trine with spiritual Neptune and energizing Mars.

I FORGET, WHAT'S A TRINE AGAIN? A trine is when a natal chart is divided three ways and forms a 120° angle. A trine planetary aspect occurs when two planets or more are in the same element, such as air, fire, water, or earth. When this happens, these planets are working toward the same outcome. If you check your birth chart and notice the trine aspect, you may find a lot of blessings and light where those planets are located.

This means it was easy for Sylvia to channel info at lightning speed. Interesting that she had her Saturn in Pisces AND Capricorn on her Twelfth House cusp. I think this was something that she was fearful and embarrassed about for quite some time. Wherever we have Capricorn and Saturn in our chart is where we are terribly insecure and fearful. But over the years we focus on it and work it, and it soon becomes our shiniest asset. Sylvia was blessed with Mars next to Neptune. Mars activates whatever it touches and next to Neptune—the ruler of her money house—Sylvia did indeed have loads of highly intuitive abilities.

Next up on the list is celebrity psychic James Van Praagh. James also has his Sun placed in the Eighth House next to intense Pluto and communicative Mercury. His Sun is also beautifully aspected with sensitive and creative Neptune, which resides in his career house along with lucky Jupiter. By the way, Jupiter expands whatever it touches and this indicates James's Neptunian nature is definitely on overdrive here. His moon is in Sag, like Sylvia's, and resides in the deeply spiritual

Twelfth House of hidden things. Interesting to note that while James has an empty house of communication, it is ruled by Pisces. This means Neptune rules his house of speech, and since Neptune is located in James's career realm, he gets his fame from talking. And that's exactly what he does. He speaks to the dead. Now let's look at John Edward, not the ex-politician, but the über-famous psychic medium.

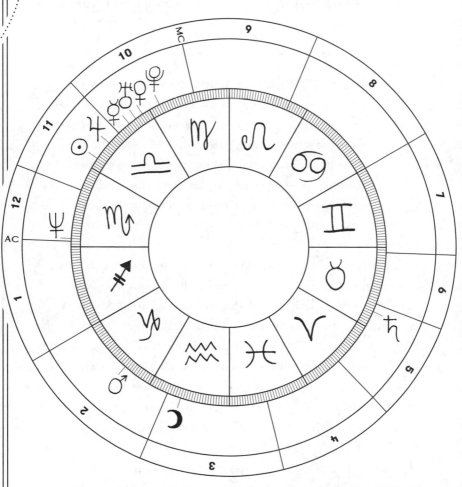

John is a Libra with a Scorpio Rising and his Moon in Aquarius. John's Eighth and Fourth houses are interestingly empty, but both houses are water-ruled, and he also has Neptune smack on his Ascendant for extra-deep intuitive abilities. His Sun sits in the Eleventh

House, so John really loves working with groups of people, and his Moon in the Third House means he needs to communicate. Look at John's Mercury in his career house. In fact, John has a packed career house, so he's no slouch when it comes to work. But it's his beautiful Mercury in Libra aligned with the planet of shock and surprise, Uranus, that is his greatest supernatural component. This means that John can download and access information at rapid speed. It's near Venus too, so his words are graceful and beautiful. See how all three planets are in a beautiful trine (a good aspect) with his Moon in the Third House? And that Moon is also linked with his spiritual Neptune on his Ascendant. It's basically his persona to be a medium! The fact that the ruler of his chart, Pluto, is in the Tenth House of career means he wouldn't do well with anything less. His abilities MUST be on display!

Truthfully there are loads of psychic indicators in a person's chart. Neptune is a big one. But Neptune can also be an indicator of a substance abuse problem. Neptune is, after all, the planet of escape—it's your decision which way you want to use it! Remember, astrology is all about free will. Good Neptune is metaphysical, musical, and artistic. Lower-vibe Neptune is pills, alcohol, and hallucinogenics. We all have Neptune somewhere; use it wisely.

CONCLUSION

Thank you for going on this journey with me! I hope you enjoyed it as much as I did, and I hope you revisit this book often. My wish is that it will assist you on your own astrological journey and help you find the life the universe wants you to live. Also remember that in many ways the placement of your planets is a result of karma, forcing your spirit to reconcile with decisions and consequences from past lives. Living your destiny now isn't going to just help you have the most fulfilling existence you can have—it also sets you up for karmic success in your next lives.

Learning about the houses, planets, and signs takes time and patience, not so easy for you fire signs out there. I recommend you study yourself, your friends and family, and often! Go ahead, drive everyone crazy with your newfound astrological insight. And don't worry if you make mistakes. That's all part of the process! The best advice I can give you is to *listen*. Observe and tune in to your "clients." Let their presence inform your readings. Life is hard enough, so remember to be delicate and tactful with your fresh new knowledge.

Remember, while you might have destiny and karmic baggage, you also have free will. Knowledge is power, and integrating the cosmos into your choices will help you find the life you were born to live.

ACKNOWLEDGMENTS

F irst and foremost, thank you to everyone who picked up this book and decided to expand their knowledge of astrology. It's a magical thing to connect with the heavens, and I salute you on your journey.

Thank you so much to my editors, Lea Taddonio and Hannah Robinson; there's no way this book would exist without these two! And to the entire team at Simon and Schuster and Tiller Press, Michael Andersen, Lauren Ollerhead, and Molly Pieper, thank you. And many thanks to Nicole Resciniti and Kim Falconer for trusting me with this book. Kim, I am forever in your debt!

Thank you to all the astrologers alive and deceased who've taught me so much and passed on such wise words of wisdom and experience. Jean Norman, Kim Falconer, and the especially the late Debbi Kempton-Smith—my teacher and my mentor. I hope you're dancing up a storm somewhere near Jupiter!

Thank you to all my friends and family who showed up with words of encouragements and support. To Liam and Ivy who spent their quarantine glued to screens while Mom locked herself in her studio—thank you. And thank you to David, who always makes life extra sparkly.

ABOUT
THE AUTHOR

RACHEL STUART-HAAS is a professional artist and astrologer who currently lives in Louisiana. She earned her BFA in Design/Illustration from the Kansas City Art Institute in Kansas City, Missouri. Since then, Rachel has focused her time and energy on producing one-of-a-kind paintings that portray her intuition toward the obvious and the ethereal. She has been fascinated with astrology since she first laid eyes on Linda Goodman's *Love Signs* in the eighth grade, and after years of working with top astrologers, Rachel launched her own practice, with clients that span the globe. Rachel lives with her husband, David, their children, Ivy and Liam, and her devoted basset hound, Louie.

Visit her online at RachelStuartHaas.com.